Roseann Ettinger

50s Popular Fashions

for Men, Women, Boys, & Girls

With Price Guide

Schiffer Publishing Ltd

77 Lower Valley Road, Atglen, PA 19310

Dedication

This book is dedicated to the loving memory of my nephew, John V. Rodino, who died this past Christmas Eve at the delicate age of 20.

Rayon necktie with hand-painted portrait of author's mother, Marie Rodino. The polka dot rayon scarf and pillbox hat is the exact set she was wearing in the photograph, seated next to the author's father, Vito Rodino. This picture was taken in Jack Dempseys in New York City in 1950.

Printed in Hong Kong

We are interested in hearing from authors with book ideas on related topics.

Published by Schiffer Publishing Ltd.
77 Lower Valley Road
Atglen, PA 19310
Please write for a free catalog.
This book may be purchased from the publisher.
Please include $2.95 postage.
Try your bookstore first.

Library of Congress Cataloging-in-Publication Data

Ettinger, Roseann.
    50s popular fashions for men, women, boys & girls / Roseann Ettinger.
        p.   cm.
    Includes bibliographical references and index.
    ISBN 0-88740-724-2 (pbk.)
    1. Costume--United States--History--20th century. 2. Fashion--United States--History--20th century. 3. Dress accessories--United States--History--20th century. I. Title. II. Title: Fifties popular fashions for men, women, boys & Girls.
GT615.E88   1995
391'.009'045--dc20   94-38470
                                    CIP

Contents

Acknowledgments

This book would not have been possible without the enthusiastic efforts of Leslie Bockol, Jeff Snyder and Nancy Schiffer. Changing those wire mannequins was not an easy task! Thank you so much. As always, I must thank my children Clint and Amber for taking time out of their schedules to watch their baby sister Alexandra. And to my husband Terry, your patience is definitely a virtue.

The man's white dress shirt is accented with small black pin-stripes and a center panel of satin with larger black stripes running vertically. The label reads "Elderado Casuals". Black gabardine slacks with a pleated front are used here. The rayon necktie is extremely special because it is a hand-painted portrait of the author's mother on her honeymoon in 1950. Looking closely at the portrait, notice that she is wearing the same rayon hat and scarf with white polka dots that the mannequin is wearing along with her blue rayon suit.

Introduction

So many distinct changes occurred in the fashion industry in the 1950s that it is impossible to capture the entire essence of the decade in one volume. The "New Look" in fashions which is credited to fashion designer Christian Dior, sparked the beginnings of modern-day costume for women in February of 1947. Sadly for some, however, this new look marked the beginning of the end of extravagant Paris couture. Social and economic influences became more important and inspirations were drawn from sources other than Paris. American style began to stand on its own after World War II.

Fashion Designers

During the 1940s, clothing was lacking in ornamentation due to war restrictions. A boxy silhouette with padded shoulders was the norm. Christian Dior's "New Look" in fashion incorporated softening of the silhouette and un-boxing the shoulders by removing the shoul-der pads. A return to femininity was evidenced with Dior's dresses, suits and coats designed with fitted bodices and flowing full skirts incorporating yards and yards of fabric. Foundation garments, particularly the boned and laced waist-cincher was a big part of this new look, creating the so-called "waspie waist". Each year, Dior created two new lines, one for Spring and one for Fall. In 1951, the Princess Line evolved. The H-Line came into existence in 1954 and by 1955, the A-and the Y-Lines were created. Fashionable tunic dresses appeared in 1956 and the chemise dress in 1957, although credit for the loose-fitting chemise belongs to Spanish-born designer Cristobal Balenciaga. After the untimely death of Dior in 1957, his protégé, Yves Saint Laurent launched his first line in 1958. This was the Trapeze Line.

Another influential designer of the 1950s was Coco Chanel who reopened her fashion house in 1954 bringing the public designs very reminiscent of her earlier works of the 1920s and the 1930s. Collarless suits, later referred to as "Chanel Suits" were the height of fashion by the end of the decade. Other popular designers of the decade include Hubert de Givenchy, Elsa Schiaparelli, Jacques Fath, Pauline Trigere, Hattie Carnegie, Nettie Rosenstein and Claire McCardell.

Ready-to-Wear

Besides the fabulous designer labels of the 1950s, the ready-to-wear fashion industry became big business. More people were unable to pay high prices for high fashion. Mass produced garments were offered through mail-order companies such as Sears, Montgomery Ward, Spiegel, National Bellas Hess, Lane Bryant, Aldens and many more. Designer clothing was still available and consistently advertised in the top fashion magazines. Major department stores across the country such as Bergdorf Goodman, I. Magnin, Julius Garfinkle, Bonwit Teller, Lord & Taylor, Marshall Field and Saks Fifth Avenue sold dresses, coats and suits with designer labels. Other popular labels from the period were Lilli Ann of San Francisco and Jonathan Logan. The average consumer, however, relied on mail-order or off-the-rack spin-offs of designer wares.

Teens

The 1950s was also the time when designing clothes for teens was a separate enterprise and certain designers and manufacturers catered to the whims of the young adult. Department stores opened separate departments for teen fashion. This was unheard of a decade earlier. Young ladies had their own money to spend, and out of rebellion, some did not want to look or dress like their mothers. Many different styles emerged for the age group between 16 and 25. Out of a need to be independent, young adults were influenced by Rock'n'Roll and Hollywood film stars. Young girls known as "Bobby-soxers" were common, as well as the "Sweater Girls" who wanted to look like Jane Russell or Marilyn Monroe. Casual campus-style clothing was popular as well as the avant-garde Beatnik who wore black tights and oversized sweaters.

Teenage boys were influenced by James Dean, Marlon Brando and Elvis Presley. Blue jeans, tee shirts and leather jackets were widely seen and DA (duck's ass) hair styles were common. The casual campus-style Ivy League look was also a part of the fashion scene for young men.

Collecting

The fashions of the fifties offer the collector a wide range to choose from. The most coveted designer clothing from the period is often too expensive for the novice collector, although occasionally, an affordable piece can be found at auctions, vintage clothing stores, thrift shops or flea markets. Off-the-rack fashions of the fifties are easier to find and not nearly as costly as the designer pieces. Some collectors are very specialized and only collect certain categories—for instance, Hawaiian shirts, hand-painted neckties, western clothing, poodle skirts, rayon dresses or Lilli Ann suits. Whatever one chooses to collect, the Fabulous Fifties is a very good place to begin because the variety of fashion produced for men, women and children was endless and is still readily found in today's market.

Collecting and wearing vintage clothing has become extremely popular in the last ten years. Movie stars, rock stars and many other celebrities wear or collect vintage clothing. Fashion designers seek examples from past eras to recreate modern versions. Vintage clothing is used in movies, TV commercials and magazine ads. The stigma once attached to wearing "Old Clothes" no longer exists. Vintage clothing is for people who want to be different, it is for those who appreciate its quality and workmanship, and it is definitely suited for those who are not led by what everyone else is wearing. Is it not popular today for a bride to wear her mother's or grandmother's wedding gown? Or Junior to come home from college and borrows dad's old Stetson hat? The quality and workmanship was excellent; the clothing has survived the test of time.

This book will enable you to identify clothing styles for men, women and children that was popular throughout the 1950s and familiarize you with the fabrics that were used to make these garments.

Finding mint condition items still retaining their original packaging is getting harder to find all the time. Because of their scarcity, the prices are escalating. With this in mind, beware that reproductions are beginning to appear. The novelty and western clothing that has been photographed for this book is genuine. Uncovered in a Philadelphia dry goods store, it had been packed away for over 40 years.

Combed cotton halters and princess-style dress fashioned for the 1955 Summer season.

Polished cotton shirtwaist dresses, in brown and blue, with contrasting vinyl belts, styled by Fruit of the Loom.

Dresses

In the first half of the 1950s, dresses for women, especially belted shirtwaist dresses with full flowing skirts were tremendously in vogue. In the Spring of 1951, the Spiegel catalog boasted that "Sheers were Top Fashion News." Sheer rayon chiffon, sheer rayon marquisette and sheer pure silk organdy were headliners. Sweetheart necklines, shirtwaist tucks and capelet collars were extremely stylish. Slim line casual dresses with lace trim were also being offered in butcher rayon which was "cool and crisp as linen." Exciting print dresses, especially florals, were made of rayon crepe which resembled silk and had excellent draping qualities. Certain characteristics of 1940s dresses were still somewhat visible in the fashion of the early 1950s. For instance, peplums on dresses and suits were often seen but as the decade progressed, the peplums were beginning to get smaller, and by the end of the decade, they were gone altogether.

Blue and white cotton sundress with matching bolero jacket by Fruit of the Loom.

More cotton sundresses with matching bolero jackets made by Majestic.

Halter and V-neck dresses made of woven-tuck rayon "...That's Linen-Crisp", Montgomery Ward, 1953.

"Dressy Cotton Sheers for Day or Evening" was the heading for these dresses offered for sale from Wards in 1955.

Cotton dress with scenic print by Fruit of the Loom.

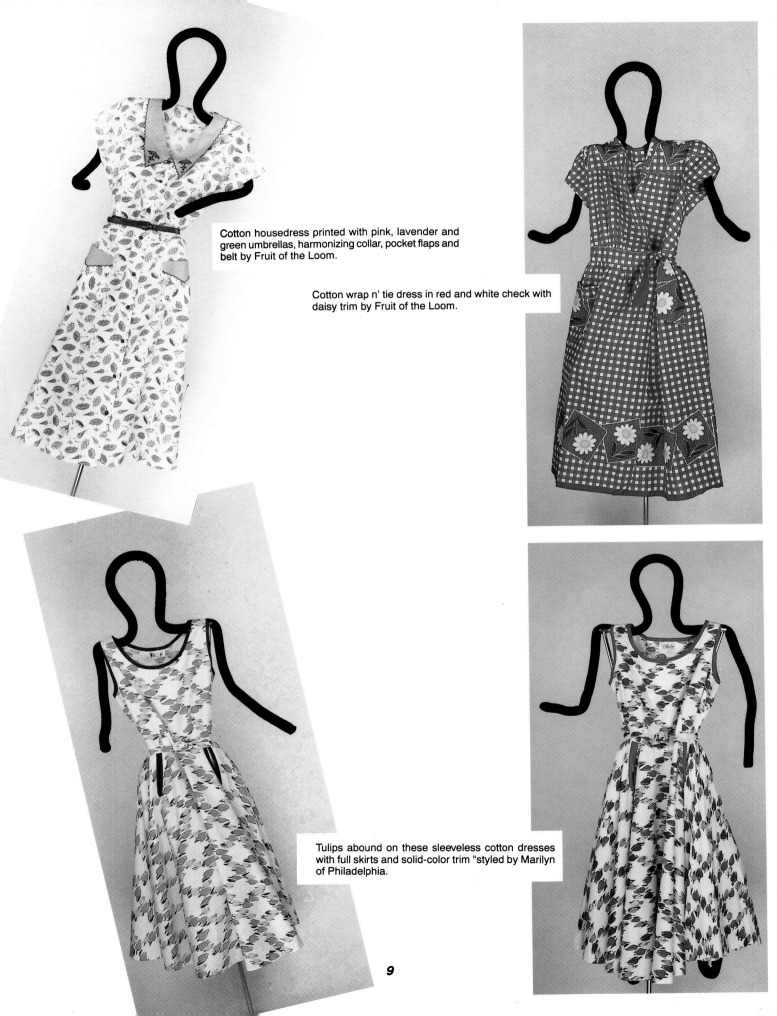

Cotton housedress printed with pink, lavender and green umbrellas, harmonizing collar, pocket flaps and belt by Fruit of the Loom.

Cotton wrap n' tie dress in red and white check with daisy trim by Fruit of the Loom.

Tulips abound on these sleeveless cotton dresses with full skirts and solid-color trim "styled by Marilyn of Philadelphia.

9

Printed cotton housedress with bright yellow trim, black buttons and belted sash by Fruit of the Loom.

Ladies wrap-around dress in printed cotton with large apple applique. Original tag on garment reads "Cotton de Oro, Quality in Fashion, 100% Cotton, Balnard Fabrics.

Wrap-around dress of cotton crepe, label reads "Fashioned by Kenrose". Original tag on garment reads "Glama Crepe, needs no ironing, quick drying, A Lowenstein Fabric".

Coordinates became extremely popular during the 1950s. This four piece ensemble consists of gathered full skirt, sleeveless blouse, capri pants and Bermuda shorts made of printed cotton by Fruit of the Loom.

Cotton peasant-style dress with leaf print and black trim "Styled by Marilyn of Philadelphia".

Cotton printed sundress with white eyelet trim, no label.

Black cotton sundress with multi-colored polka dots "Styled by Marilyn of Philadelphia". Plastic necklace by Trifari.

A harlequin print covers this sleeveless cotton day dress with piped trim "Styled by Marilyn of Philadelphia".

Cotton day dress printed with red and yellow scottie dogs, red trim and belt, "Styled by Marilyn of Philadelphia".

Pink and black floral printed day dress with scroll embroidery by Fruit of the Loom.

Tiny white buttons are printed on this cotton sundress with matching bolero jacket made by Fruit of the Loom.

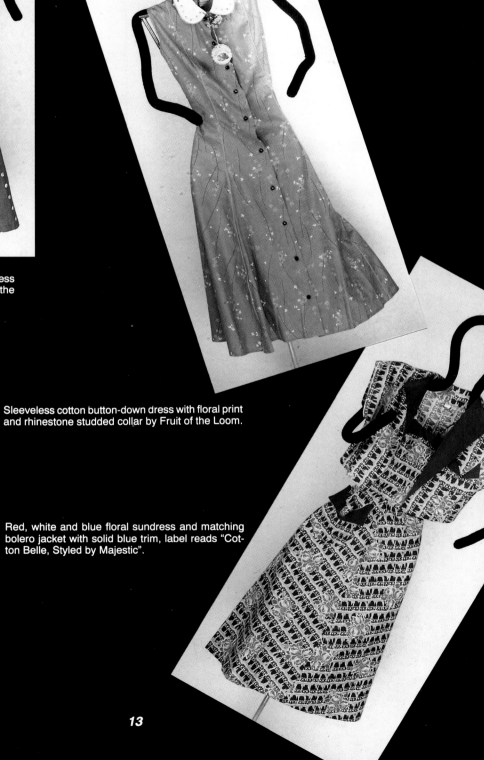

Sleeveless cotton button-down dress with floral print and rhinestone studded collar by Fruit of the Loom.

Red, white and blue floral sundress and matching bolero jacket with solid blue trim, label reads "Cotton Belle, Styled by Majestic".

Viking ships decorate this two-piece ensemble made by Fruit of the Loom. This outfit was also made in green and blue.

Two-piece Dresses

Dresses made with rows of horizontal tucks were extremely popular, not to mention they were flattering to the figure. Decorative scroll embroidery or passementerie was applied to dresses and suit jackets. Two-piece suit dresses were also stylish made with either a sundress and a bolero jacket or a short sleeve, belted dress and fitted jacket, sometimes accented with a peplum.

Navy blue and black, being advertised as the "most flattering colors" for the Spring of 1951, were utilized to the fullest with dresses and suits made of rayon crepe, rayon faille, rayon taffeta and puckered nylon.

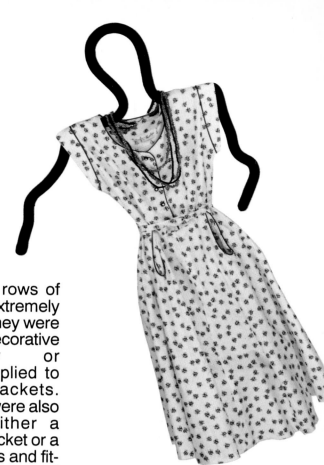

Yellow printed day dress with cap sleeves and button-down front "Styled by Marilyn of Philadelphia".

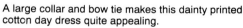

A large collar and bow tie makes this dainty printed cotton day dress quite appealing.

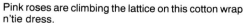

Pink roses are climbing the lattice on this cotton wrap n'tie dress.

14

A stylish contrast was made here with the use of small and large flowers on this cotton, belted sundress. The paper tag promotes the appealing feature of a two-inch hem.

Orlon

By 1953, women's fashions were made of the newest wonder fabrics such as nylon, acetate and Orlon. An advertisement for Orlon found in the *Woman's Home Companion* stated that Orlon was a "New blueprint in fashions with a care-free future!" The ad went on to say that "The young idea in clothes-as in homes-is to look smart with the least upkeep. And DuPont Orlon acrylic fiber makes it possible with women's suits and dresses that have a warm, soft feel...an extravagant look - but new and better behavior. Their press is not just for today - but for tomorrow and tomorrow. They're neat-keeping, pleat-keeping...and keep their first day look with just easy care."

Printed cotton day dress with harmonizing collar, cuffs and pocket flaps made by Fruit of the Loom.

Checkerboard print dress with contrasting collar, pockets, belt and buttons by Fruit of the Loom.

Pink cotton dress with black lace print and light pink trim, label reads "Cotton City".

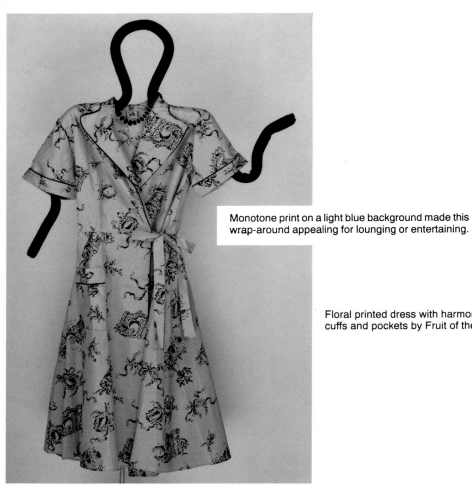

Monotone print on a light blue background made this wrap-around appealing for lounging or entertaining.

Floral printed dress with harmonizing trim on collar, cuffs and pockets by Fruit of the Loom.

Suit dress, princess-style dress and coat dress of silk shantung and cotton & rayon faille, Wards, 1955.

Sleeveless printed shirtwaist dress, label reads "Orange Maid".

16

The Chemise coat dress made of rayon, cotton and acetate, advertised for sale in 1958.

Cotton printed day dress with harmonizing sailor collar and pocket trim by Fruit of the Loom. Patch-work alligator handbag, no label.

Brown rayon dress printed with pale pink roses and green leaves, button-down front and gathered waist, no label.

Light blue rayon day-to-evening dress printed with pink roses, gathered waist, two pockets and belt, no label. Hot pink feathered pill box hat, no label.

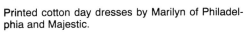
Printed cotton day dresses by Marilyn of Philadelphia and Majestic.

Two identical gabardine dresses with classic tailoring, decorated with brass studs and mother of pearl. The labels read "Created by Westover Wearables, New York".

Trio of colorful linen-like rayon dresses accented with lace and braid.

Green rayon dress with ribbon print and grosgrain ribbon trim by Cày Artley. The braided and sequined hat has no label.

Belted dress made of rayon crepe, hand-decorated with milkglass beads forming tiny umbrellas and floral rosettes.

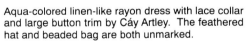

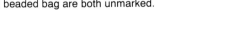

Aqua-colored linen-like rayon dress with lace collar and large button trim by Cáy Artley. The feathered hat and beaded bag are both unmarked.

Lovely printed dress made of pure silk accented with sequins. The hat is made of satin with metallic thread decorations, no label.

Purple linen-like rayon dress decorated with white embroidered flowers. Label reads "Styled by Lenny".

Mustard-colored linen-like rayon dress accented with delicate lace inserts. Original tag reads "Cáy Artley, Wonder-Ful Lin". Straw hat with floral decoration by Christian Dior; Lucite handbag in the shape of a suitcase by Stylecraft, Miami.

Textured and printed nylon shirtwaist dress by "The House of Shroyers"; felt and net hat by Véola Modes, New York.

Nylon

Nylon by DuPont was another popular choice for summer dresses, blouses and lingerie and very little care was needed to keep that fresh and crisp look. Nylon washed easily, dried quickly and needed little or no ironing. Many varieties were available including plain or fancy puckered nylon, part nylon sheer, flocked nylon, nylon pique and Orlon and nylon blends. They were used consistently throughout the decade.

Gray rayon dress with contrasting green and white stripe trim on collar, buttonholes and pockets was made by Fruit of the Loom. The two-toned green velvet turban-style hat has no label.

Green and white printed dress with large collar, velvet buttons and black flower. Original tag reads "A fabric of Chromspun Eastman color-locked acetate containing crystal chromspun".

Black rayon shirtwaist dress with large leaf print, label reads "The House of Shroyers, Built by A Father and Four Sons, Founded May 2, 1914, Shamokin, Pennsylvania". White straw hat with pink flowers, label reads "Gwenn Pennington Exclusive, New York

Floral printed dress made of rayon with v-neck collar and black grosgrain belt. The beads and the hat are contemporary and although this dress is almost fifty years old, it too looks contemporary.

Cotton

Cotton, always being a good choice for plain or printed summer dresses, was used tremendously throughout the 1950s. Many varieties of cotton were available. Embossed cotton, cotton broadcloth, cotton batiste, polished cotton, chambray, cotton taffeta and cotton plisse were a few of the favorites.

Red and white polka dot shirtwaist dress of rayon crepe, label reads "Exclusively by Cáy Artley". Accessories include a red felt hat, imitation cordé bag and white beads by Marvella.

Brown rayon dress printed with flowers and silhouette medallions, designed with shawl collar, belted waist and tiered skirt, no label.

Coffee-colored rayon dress with light blue flowers and black abstract designs, label reads "Pat Perkins".

Gray linen-like rayon dress with red and white abstract designs, label reads "Fashioned by Kenchester Frocks". The red and black straw hat is contemporary.

A-line and Y-line

In 1955, dress styles began to change to a certain degree with the creation of the A-line and the Y-line, but that did not mean that previous styles did not exist. Belted shirtwaist dresses with full flowing skirts were still in vogue and constantly advertised for sale, along with the new designs featuring drop waists or Empire waists.

Burgandy shirtwaist dress of acetate/rayon by Cày Artley. Original tag reads "Matelassé fabric by Burlington Mills, 1951". Black velvet picture hat with floral decoration by Leon Hats, New York.

Abstract printed linen-like rayon dress with green piped trim. Label reads "Styled by Marilyn of Philadelphia". The feathered hat is by Deena, New York.

Printed chiffon and taffeta dress accessorized with large plateau hat made of synthetic straw offered for sale in 1957.

Jersey

In September of 1956, an article in *Family Circle* made mention of the "newly fashionable Jersey, with its many new faces" being the most exciting fabric for the fall. The article went on to say that "the new jerseys are firmly knit - an asset in draping and tailoring. Textures go all the way from the soft smooth surfaces to bulky novelties and tweed types. Because of their unusual style interest, you'll find jerseys in every type of apparel." Dresses, suits, blouses and pullover tops were made of this fabric.

Floral and figural designs are seen throughout this lovely dress with drop waist dating from the late 1940s. The yellow net hat dates from the 1960s.

Silk halter dress with matching bolero jacket, label reads "Hawaiian Casuals, Made in Hawaii for The Liberty House, Honolulu". The basket-shaped purse with Lucite top has a label that reads "Simon, Made in Hong Kong"; label in gold turban-style hat reads "Norman Durand Original".

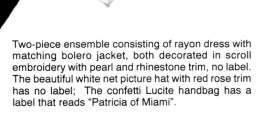

Two-piece ensemble consisting of rayon dress with matching bolero jacket, both decorated in scroll embroidery with pearl and rhinestone trim, no label. The beautiful white net picture hat with red rose trim has no label; The confetti Lucite handbag has a label that reads "Patricia of Miami".

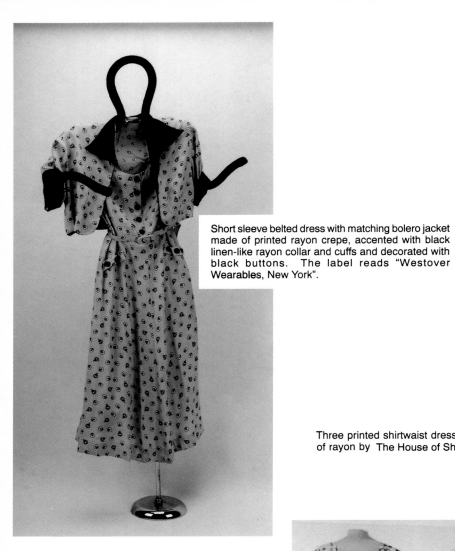

Short sleeve belted dress with matching bolero jacket made of printed rayon crepe, accented with black linen-like rayon collar and cuffs and decorated with black buttons. The label reads "Westover Wearables, New York".

Three printed shirtwaist dresses made of rayon by The House of Shroyers.

Hand-screened silk dresses offered for sale from Spiegel in 1951.

Advertised in 1953 as "Sheer Loveliness in Misses' Frocks", these dresses were made of organdy, combed cotton and cotton voile.

These charming dresses were designed by Henry Rosenfeld and sold through the Montgomery Ward catalog in 1953. They were made of nylon.

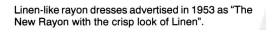

Linen-like rayon dresses advertised in 1953 as "The New Rayon with the crisp look of Linen".

Plain and puckered nylon dresses popular for the Spring and Summer season of 1953.

Novelty cotton dresses popular in the Summer of 1953.

An appliqued yoke, a vivid contrast and a bias stripe were the headliners used to describe these cotton dresses fashionable in 1953.

The cinch-belt fashion in mint green acetate crepe, Montgomery Ward, 1955.

C
12.98

A polka dot shirtwaist dress and a navy suit dress both made of crisp puckered nylon and advertised in 1953.

Advertised as "Our Newest Washable Wonder Fashions", these dresses were made of nylon and sold through Wards in 1953.

Printed dresses made of arnel & cotton and dacron & cotton, Aldens, 1959.

A bejewelled evening top made of wool, completely encrusted with sequins, beads and pearls, made in Hong Kong for The House of Gold. Accessories include turquoise satin gloves, Lucite handbag, rhinestone necklace and feathered hat by Europa, made in Belgium.

Identical cotton sundresses with matching bolero jackets designed with a brick wall pattern in brown/blue and black/yellow combinations styled by Majestic.

Empire sheath dress in black and white floral print, Wards,1957.

Full-skirted party dress of printed cotton advertised in a German fashion magazine in 1958.

Sheath

Sheath dresses were extremely fashionable in 1957 either with Empire waists or the bloused look with a belt. Tailored shirtwaist dresses were still being featured for day or evening wear. Nylon lace over taffeta was a popular combination for evening dresses. Jumpers and cotton knit tee shirt dresses were gaining in popularity at this time.

Rayon crepe dress with silver sequin decorations across the top of the dress and the bottom of the peplum.

Party dress of white chiffon with sequined bodice and satin trim.

This stunning two-piece evening ensemble is made of rayon acetate woven with metallic threads and lined in satin. The top is made with a cowl neck and a v-shaped yoke. The label reads "That Wilroy Look". The handbag was made with cut steel beads.

Rayon evening dress completely encrusted with sequins, label reads "Gene Shelly's, Dale Lin, California, Hand decorated in Hong Kong". The label in the blue feathered hat reads "Norman Durand Original".

Exquisite black net and taffeta dress fashioned with ornate ribbon art forming flowers and scroll designs, no label. Accessories include silk metallic shawl, metallic high-heeled shoes, goldtone beaded necklaces and contemporary feathered mask.

This outfit is definitely bedazzling! Black rayon evening blouse completely encrusted with beadwork in diamond and zig zag designs and black beaded fringe which covers the front and the back of the blouse. The label reads "House of Gold, Made in Hong Kong, British Crown Colony". The black crepe skirt is also decorated with black fringe. The handmade beaded bag with satin lining was made in Italy for Rosenfeld. The pillbox hat, made of black net with sequins has no label.

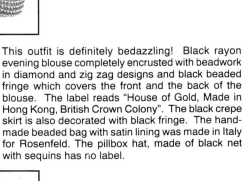

The Trapeze dress was fashionable in the late 1950s. This particular example was offered for sale from **Sears** in 1958.

An original design by Hannah Troy, this mauve evening dress was made of DuPont's Orlon and silk and advertised in *Vogue* in 1955. A footnote at the bottom of the magazine ad stated that "Orlon is DuPont's registered trademark for its acrylic fiber. DuPont makes fibers, not fabrics or garments." The jewelry was made by Kramer.

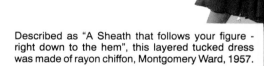

14.98

Described as "A Sheath that follows your figure - right down to the hem", this layered tucked dress was made of rayon chiffon, Montgomery Ward, 1957.

Oriental embroidered black satin evening dress with matching jacket; net hat dates from the 1960s, unmarked.

Off white silk dress made in the H-line style popularized by Christian Dior in 1954, which accentuated the bosom and dropped the waist. The dress was purchased in Saks Fifth Avenue, New York by Betty Sharp, a New York night club singer and accordion player in the mid-1950s. The large brimmed feathered hat has a label that reads "Flo-Raye, New York"; the silk shoes are unmarked.

Sheath dress with tiers of all-around tucks made of rayon and acetate, Montgomery Ward, 1953.

Cotton lace and nylon chiffon Party dress lined with rayon taffeta and advertised in *Seventeen* in 1958.

Evening dress made of hot pink and white silk chiffon with sequined bodice; pink leather shoes by Jacqueline; hot pink hat with floral decorations, no label.

The Bell Silhouette made of acetate taffeta, Sears, 1958.

This rayon dress with draped lace overskirt was offered for sale in 1953 for $13.98.

Chemise

The overall look of fashion for women dramatically changed in 1958 with the chemise dress, the trapeze dress and the bell silhouette. Harem-skirted dresses were also seen for a short time. Coat dresses remained classics as well as belted shirtwaist dresses. Jumpers were still fashionable and coordinates became the newest rage. For the holiday season of 1958, dresses and separates featured "Back Interest" for looking spectacular either coming or going. Buttons, bows, bands of satin and deep-cut necklines were a few of the special features. By 1959, bright colors such as orange, lime green, hot pink and sapphire blue made big fashion news and plain and printed coordinates remained popular.

Nylon and rayon taffeta party dresses by Doris Dodson advertised in *Seventeen* magazine in November of 1958.

Formal gowns for 1953 made of rayon and acetate tissue faille (J) and rayon chiffon with chantilly-type lace (K).

Ad for Nadine Formals in pastels and white advertised in *Seventeen* in 1958.

Evening dress of cream-colored satin with scalloped neckline, hand-decorated with bugle beads, sequins, rhinestones and hand-blown glass beads. The label reads "Hess Brothers French Room, Allentown, Pa.". The handcrafted leather shoes are marked "Marquise"; the label in the large picture hat reads "Millinery Salon, Lit Brothers, Philadelphia".

Party or Prom dresses made of nylon tulle and advertised in *Seventeen* in 1958. They were available in many colors including Legion blue, Nile green, lipstick red, golden maize, pink, black, aqua and turquoise.

Evening Gowns

Evening gowns were attractively made of brocade, satin, lame, silk and rayon in long and short forms. The basic black dress, however, always made a dynamic fashion statement for evening wear especially accented with the right accessories. Bouffant-style dresses were made of tulle, rayon chiffon and acetate and nylon lace. Ballerina length evening gowns were extremely fashionable made of nylon net decorated with nylon lace or imported French lace.

Rhinestone-studded black velvet evening dress, no label. Black velvet hat with bead and rhinestone trim; gunmetal-colored glass beaded bag by "Josef, Hand Beaded in Belgium".

Chiffon evening gown and strapless party dress **made** of nylon offered for sale from Sears in 1958.

34

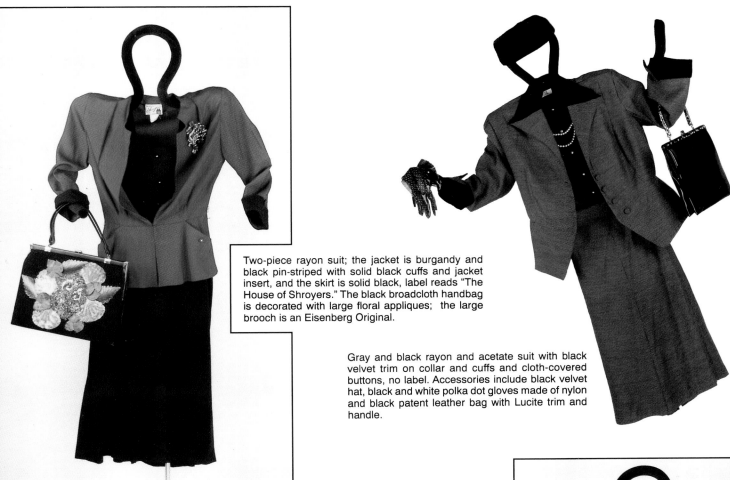

Two-piece rayon suit; the jacket is burgandy and black pin-striped with solid black cuffs and jacket insert, and the skirt is solid black, label reads "The House of Shroyers." The black broadcloth handbag is decorated with large floral appliques; the large brooch is an Eisenberg Original.

Gray and black rayon and acetate suit with black velvet trim on collar and cuffs and cloth-covered buttons, no label. Accessories include black velvet hat, black and white polka dot gloves made of nylon and black patent leather bag with Lucite trim and handle.

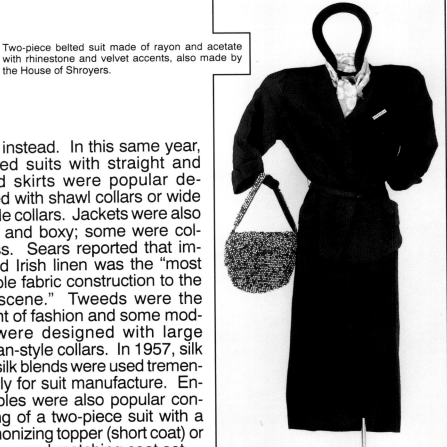

Two-piece belted suit made of rayon and acetate with rhinestone and velvet accents, also made by the House of Shroyers.

Suits

Fashionable for the fall of 1953 were tailored suits for women made of wool gabardine, rayon and acetate sheen gabardine, rayon and acetate faille and virgin wool. Silk shantung was another fine choice for suitings. Belted suit jackets were in style as well as those with double flared peplums. Special treatment was applied to jacket pockets and lapels were often rounded. Beadwork and scroll embroidery was found on dressier examples. By 1955, genuine fur was frequently used to adorn suits, coats and dresses. When fur was not actually attached to the coat or suit, large fur muffs and hats were used instead. In this same year, tailored suits with straight and flared skirts were popular designed with shawl collars or wide double collars. Jackets were also short and boxy; some were collarless. Sears reported that imported Irish linen was the "most notable fabric construction to the suit scene." Tweeds were the height of fashion and some models were designed with large puritan-style collars. In 1957, silk and silk blends were used tremendously for suit manufacture. Ensembles were also popular consisting of a two-piece suit with a harmonizing topper (short coat) or a dress and matching coat set.

Two-piece nubby-tweed suit made of rayon, acetate and wool, label reads "House of Shroyers". The belt and rhinestone buttons on flaps add to its classic styling. The navy blue sailor-style straw hat has no label.

Two-piece gold-colored suit made of imported cotton with glass buttons, label reads "Rinaldo, Ltd.". The accessorie include a feathered hat by Mary Walker, Hazleton, Pa., and a beaded handbag by Richere.

Theatre suit by Hannah Troy in Roman Holiday Red Orlon and silk. The jewelry was made by Kramer, *Vogue*, 1955.

Suit styles popular in 1953 advertised for sale from Montgomery Ward.

Classic styling is evidenced here in this suit dress with fluted trim made of "Juilliard's Kuana", a fabric with a nubby texture made of 60% silk and 40% acetate, Wards, 1953.

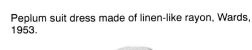

Two-piece tailored suit made of bronze-colored cotton, accented with wooden buttons, label reads "Imported cotton woven exclusively for Rinaldo Ltd.". The gold-colored sheer nylon blouse has no label; the metal basket weave handbag with Lucite top is also unmarked.

Peplum suit dress made of linen-like rayon, Wards, 1953.

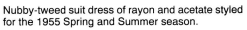

Nubby-tweed suit dress of rayon and acetate styled for the 1955 Spring and Summer season.

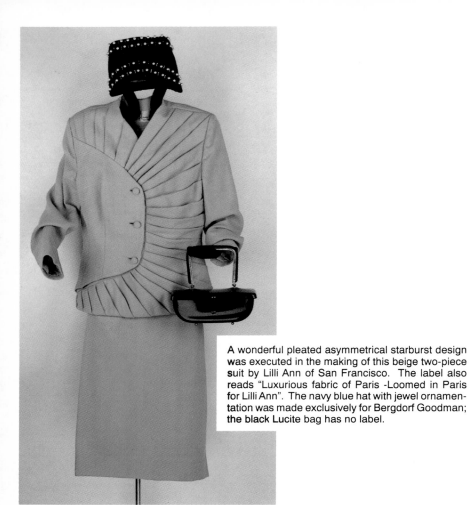

A wonderful pleated asymmetrical starburst design was executed in the making of this beige two-piece suit by Lilli Ann of San Francisco. The label also reads "Luxurious fabric of Paris -Loomed in Paris for Lilli Ann". The navy blue hat with jewel ornamentation was made exclusively for Bergdorf Goodman; the black Lucite bag has no label.

Chenille wool knit suits fashionable in 1958.

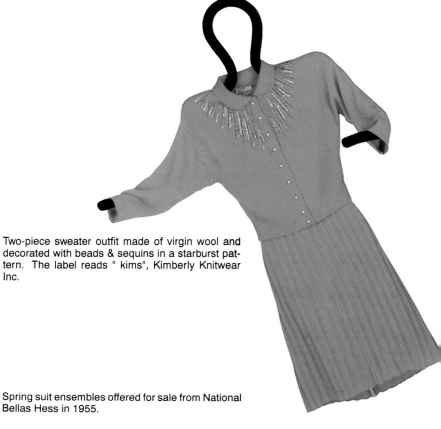

Two-piece sweater outfit made of virgin wool and decorated with beads & sequins in a starburst pattern. The label reads " kims", Kimberly Knitwear Inc.

Spring suit ensembles offered for sale from National Bellas Hess in 1955.

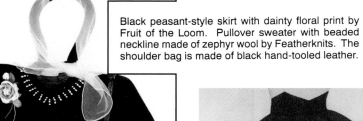

Black peasant-style skirt with dainty floral print by Fruit of the Loom. Pullover sweater with beaded neckline made of zephyr wool by Featherknits. The shoulder bag is made of black hand-tooled leather.

Slim and flared skirts for the 1959 Spring and Summer season, Aldens.

Pink, black and white daisies decorate this cotton circle skirt by Fruit of the Loom. Black Orlon sweater, accented with beadwork, made by Featherknits.

Colorful fashions made of cotton popular in 1954.

43

Floral button-down cardigan sweater by Featherknits made of Orlon acrylic. Lime-green gabardine skirt, tailored in design, with woven rust-colored plaid, no label.

Green gabardine skirt, gathered at the waist, with two imitation pockets accented with brass buttons. Very unusual white cashmere sweater hand-decorated with green and white beads forming three-dimensional grape clusters. The multi-colored caviar beaded handbag was a popular item in the 1950s.

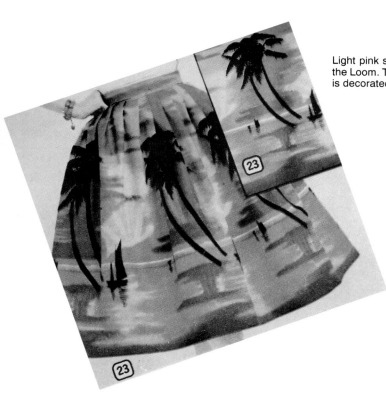

Circle skirt with a "Blazing Glow of Color" offered for sale from Aldens in 1959.

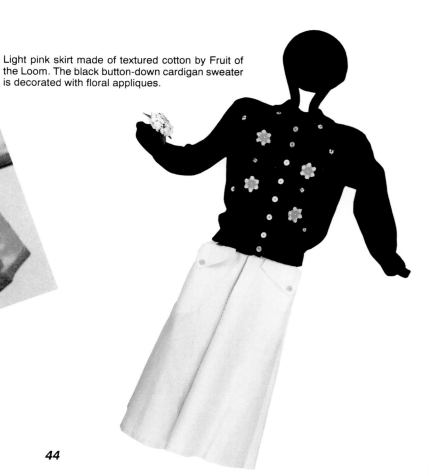

Light pink skirt made of textured cotton by Fruit of the Loom. The black button-down cardigan sweater is decorated with floral appliques.

The straight skirt with double front pleat is made of greenish-yellow rayon. The original tag reads "A Willow Sportswear Original". The lined black lambswool sweater was custom knit in Japan for Lane Bryant. It is hand decorated with multi-colored beads and pearls in floral designs.

Multi-colored horizontal stripes decorate this black permanent-pleated skirt by Fruit of the Loom; the lavender Orlon sweater was made by Featherknits.

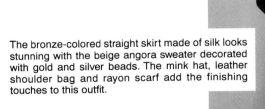

The bronze-colored straight skirt made of silk looks stunning with the beige angora sweater decorated with gold and silver beads. The mink hat, leather shoulder bag and rayon scarf add the finishing touches to this outfit.

Straight skirts made of wool fashionable in 1954.

HARMONIZED IN COLOR!
Sweater and Skirt Match-Mates
Mix or Match Them . . . All are color-keyed
to blend one with the other . . .

Mix and match separates offered for sale from
Rohde-Spencer Company in 1958.

46

The black pleated pants by Fruit of the Loom are used here with the linen-weave rayon sleeveless blouse decorated with goldtone studs on collar and pocket. The multi-colored striped sneakers are P.F. Flyers.

Green and white checked blouse accented with solid white trim and black bow is used here with black cotton belted pants both manufactured by Fruit of the Loom.

Blouses

Blouses for women, made in many fabrics, came in all shapes and styles. In the early 1950s, rayon crepe, nylon and cotton were used frequently. By 1955, Dacron was considered another wonder fiber. Similar to nylon, Dacron was easy to launder, it dried quickly and needed little or no ironing. It was the perfect choice for the fancy pleated and ruffled blouses of the period. Puckered, flocked and sheer nylon blouses came in all colors and were perfect for use with suits.

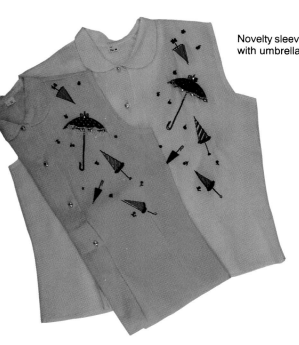

Novelty sleeveless blouses made of rayon decorated with umbrellas, rhinestones and nylon lace trim.

Yellow sleeveless blouse made of linen-like rayon decorated with umbrellas, lace and rhinestones compliments the versatile black pants by Fruit of the Loom.

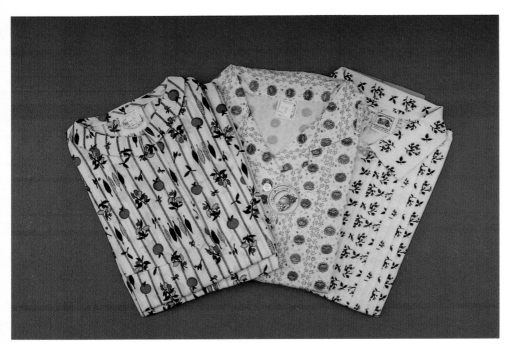

Cotton, organdy, batiste and pique were especially suited for summer use. Peasant-style blouses with flattering necklines were fashionable as well as tailored styles made of imported silk. Collars ranged from the popular Peter Pan style to the wide wing collars found on men's shirts. Jewel necklines were always considered classic fashion and popular throughout the decade. Dolman sleeves, short sleeves, cap sleeves and sleeveless versions were found everywhere. Special treatment was applied such as appliques, lace, bows, embroidery, pleating, tucking, shirring, studding with rhinestones, hand beading or hand painting.

Fruits and flowers decorate these cotton blouses made by Fruit of the Loom.

Dacron and sheer nylon blouses by Jack Daniels.

Sleeveless cotton blouses designed with a red and blue diamond pattern and solid white trim.

Blouses made of nylon batiste and linen-like rayon, Wards, 1953.

Cotton blouses made in a variety of styles for the 1953 Spring and Summer season.

Variety of blouses fashionable in 1954 in solids, prints, checks, ginghams and stripes.

Novelty blouses made of nylon, organdy and cotton, Wards, 1953.

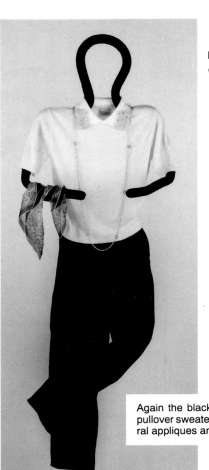

Blouses made of Jersey, Arnel Tricot and Dacron crepe offered for sale in 1958.

Again the black pants are used with a pink Orlon pullover sweater with white collar decorated with floral appliques and rhinestone trim by Featherknits.

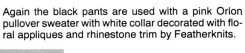

The bright yellow rayon blouse with floral appliques and rhinestone trim is quite bedazzling. The handbag is made of dyed Cobra.

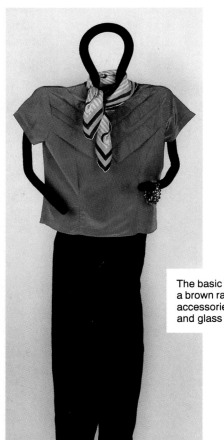

The basic black gabardine pants are used here with a brown rayon blouse with diagonal box pleats. The accessories include a silk scarf with mandolin print and glass beaded bracelet by De Mario.

Two tailored blouses made of white and ecru lace are studded with multi-colored rhinestones, label reads "Starmaker".

A white rayon blouse with scroll embroidery and rhinestone trim at the yoke is used here with the basic black pants. The label in the blouse reads "A Winnie Kaye Original." Accessories include a black felt hat, tapestry handbag and Mother of Pearl bangle bracelet.

The versatile black gabardine pants are used here with this lovely silk pullover top encrusted with black and red beads. The sequined shoulder bag is contemporary and it was made by DeLill.

Black cotton pants and black cotton blouse with white scalloped stitched trim were both made by Fruit of the Loom.

51

Wonderful black knit top with pearl trim and metallic thread decorations around neckline, label reads "Erte Original." The black and white plateau style hat with abstract designs has no label. Pearl and rhinestone clutch bag was made in Japan.

A casual yet elegant silhouette is achieved with this black lace top made with scalloped neckline and sleeves and the basic black gabardine pants. The contemporary shoulder bag made of gunmetal-colored beads is by DeLill.

Sleeveless wool evening top completely covered with sequins, beads and pearls. The label reads "Sweater Bee, Made in Hong Kong, Every style a Honey, 100% wool". Accessories include a clear Lucite handbag studded with clear rhinestones and a black hat with feather and rhinestone trim, no label.

Lovely off-white pullover made of rayon boucle delicately trimmed with a lacy braid, label reads "It's a Gem Creation." The black cotton pants were made by Fruit of the Loom and the scottie dog print scarf is made of rayon.

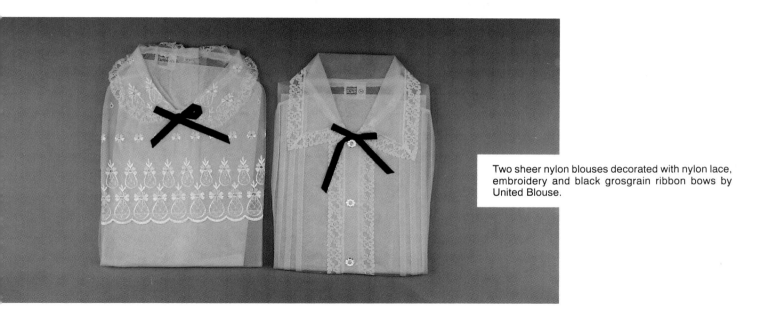

Two sheer nylon blouses decorated with nylon lace, embroidery and black grosgrain ribbon bows by United Blouse.

A sheer nylon blouse is used under this evening sweater made of virgin wool with a mink collar. The label in the sweater reads "Bernard Altman". The tapestry bag with leather handle has no label, while the fur and feathered hat reads Jean Arlett.

The brown pleated pants made of gabardine look charming with this black cashmere sweater decorated with gold beadwork. The gold sequined clutch bag adds the finishing touch.

Sweaters

Neatly tailored sweaters made of nylon, Australian zephyr wool, virgin worsted wool, cotton, and rayon and cotton boucle were fashioned in the early 1950s. Button-down cardigans, fitted pullovers and v-neck Hollywood-style coat sweaters were the rage. As the decade progressed, Orlon became one of the most popular fibers used for knitted sweaters. Tweed sweaters were made of nylon flecked with wool. New colors were introduced for Spring and for Fall. Holiday season was the time for dressy sweaters made of Angora and cashmere with hand-beaded decorations. Mohair was also introduced in the 1950s. Sweaters were trimmed with fur, metallic braid, beads, sequins, floral appliques, lace and embroidery. Adaptable and versatile sweater shrugs with dolman sleeves were popular throughout the decade.

Black pleated gabardine pants by Fruit of the Loom are used here with a white button-down sweater accented with black beadwork, no label.

Black and white striped cotton pedal pushers were made by Fruit of the Loom. The black Orlon sweater was decorated with metallic thread, label reads "100% Orlon Acrylic fiber, Helen Sue, B&B Sweater Mills, New York City". The black felt hat with tassels has no label.

A light blue cashmere sweater decorated with blue beadwork is used here with black gabardine pants. Woolen gloves and hat with fur trim makes this outfit quite seasonal.

Black pleated pants by Fruit of the Loom, white cashmere sweater decorated with pearl trim, and the straw cloche hat was made by Dowa, New York.

Ladies' cotton knit tops in black, white and red trimmed with sequins, ribbon and metallic threads.

HOLLYWOOD-TYPE COAT SWEATER
in 100% Virgin Wool or Orlon

L

	Wool Sizes 36 to 46	Orlon Sizes 36 to 46
ig g 94	$4 44	$6 49

Silver gray		Rico green
Navy blue	Luster blue	Wine flame

A button-down cardigan called the Hollywood-type coat sweater was fashionable in the 1950s. This example was offered for sale in 1955.

Beige angora sweater hand beaded and embroidered by Beauty Art Embroidery Co., Made in Hong Kong.

Three button-down sweaters made of nylon trimmed with metallic threads by Bee-Lon, B & B Sweater Mills, New York City.

STYLED FOR WARMTH AND BEAUTY

FULL FASHIONED IN ORLON OR WOOL

Full fashioned at armholes to give you a more perfect, more flattering fit. Orlon Sweaters hand wash beautifully, dry quickly. Need no blocking. Wool sweaters in 100% virgin zephyr wool are extra soft and warm. Hand washable . . shrink-resistant.

A Virgin Wool $3.98
B Virgin Orlon $3.78
F Orlon $6.90
D Virgin Orlon $4.49
G Orlon $4.90
C Virgin Worsted Wool $5.80 initial extra
E Virgin Orlon $5.49

Shrugs, pullovers and cardigans made of Orlon or wool advertised for sale in 1955.

Eleven Orlon acrylic button-down cardigan sweaters in a rainbow of colors by Featherknits.

Calypso print shirt, Jamaica shorts, pedal pushers and capri pants advertised as "Summer Pairables designed with that West Coast Dash" offered for sale in 1959 from Aldens.

Sport Clothes

Casual sport clothing for women consisted of Bermuda shorts, short shorts, slacks, halter and camisole tops, swimsuits, sunsuits and culottes. Pedal pushers, which came below the knee, were extremely popular in the early 1950s. Capri pants, which came above the ankle, were fashionable in the late 1950s. Dungarees for women were popular in the early 1950s made of sanforized (maximum fabric shrinkage 1%) cotton. In 1955, the "New Denim," which was made of rayon and acetate, was available in a wide range of fashion colors. Mexican and Indian influences were visible in peasant-style clothing. Blouses were designed with off the shoulder portrait necklines and squaw dresses also consisted of elasticized necklines and tiered-effect skirts decorated with rick-rack trim. In 1957, Montgomery Ward advertised casual clothes with "many looks from many lands." Items like "French Inspired Overblouses," "Italian Gondolier Jackets," "Jamaican-type Bandana Print Blouses," and "Caribbean Look Shorts" were offered. Western-style clothing was also popular for women with embroidered shirts taking top billing.

Summer play clothes in cool cotton prints, Aldens, 1959.

Charcoal gray denim play clothes sold through Montgomery Ward in 1953. This durable denim fabric was also available in lilac, medium brown, faded blue and dawn pink.

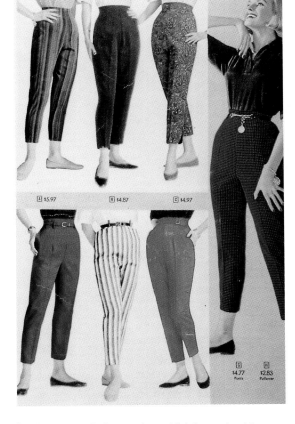

Capri pants made in a variety of fabrics and sold through Sears in 1958.

Play clothes fashioned from watercolor cotton denims offered for sale from Spiegel in 1951.

Popular styles in swimwear for the Summer of 1955.

Night-wear Lingerie

Glamorous nightwear for women consisted of gowns made of rayon crepe, knit rayon with satiny stripes, nylon tricot, acetate and rayon crepe and acetate tricot. Cotton plisse was extremely common throughout the decade and gowns, pajamas and robes were made of this fabric in plain or printed styles. Cotton plisse was another wash-and-wear fabric of the 1950s. Pajamas were man-tailored or mandarin-style.

Another cotton quilted bathrobe with aquamarine background and lavender roses and piped heart-shaped pockets by Fruit of the Loom.

Quilted bathrobes and brunch coats fashionable in 1958.

Navy blue crinkle cotton duster with gold plaid collar, cuffs and pockets by Fruit of the Loom.

Collarless and Peter Pan collar styles were also popular. By 1955, Dacron and nylon blends created nightgowns with permanent pleated designs. Lounge and sleep sets were fashionable consisting of pajamas and matching robes. Robes came in all shapes and sizes. Dusters were stylish as well as tailored coachman-style robes. Brunch coats and wraparounds were popular throughout the decade. Quilted cotton, embossed cotton, chenille, rayon, satin, silk, acetate, flannel and terry cloth were used. Robes made of Dacron and nylon were advertised as "Miracle Robes" in 1955 because they were luxurious yet economical with features like "wash, drip dry, needs no ironing and resists rips and wrinkles."

Trio of leisure wear garments in checkerboard prints with gold and black striped collars, pocket flaps and rope belt by Fruit of the Loom.

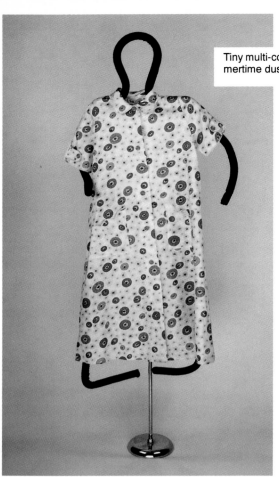

Tiny multi-colored parasols create a whimsical summertime duster made by Fruit of the Loom.

Mandarin-style robe made of teal-colored crinkle cotton decorated with black trim and poodle applique on side pocket by Fruit of the Loom.

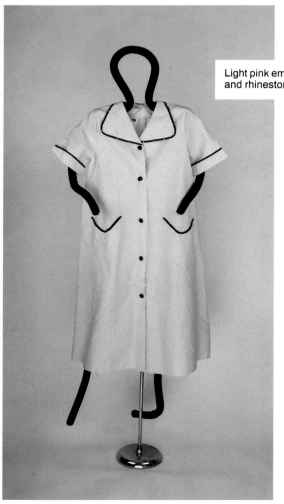

Light pink embossed cotton bathrobe with black trim and rhinestone studded collar by Fruit of the Loom.

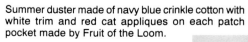

Summer duster made of navy blue crinkle cotton with white trim and red cat appliques on each patch pocket made by Fruit of the Loom.

64

Another printed cotton quilted robe with scalloped front and piped trim by Fruit of the Loom Inc., Providence, Rhode Island.

Summer robe of teal crinkle cotton with black cat appliques by Fruit of the Loom.

Novelty prints were common throughout the 1950s. This cotton quilted double-breasted robe by Fruit of the Loom is covered with tiny hourglasses. The yellow piping and large patch pockets add to the overall look.

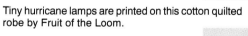

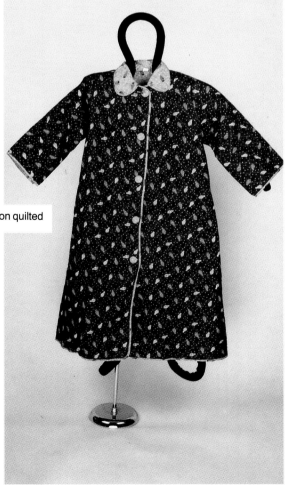

Tiny hurricane lamps are printed on this cotton quilted robe by Fruit of the Loom.

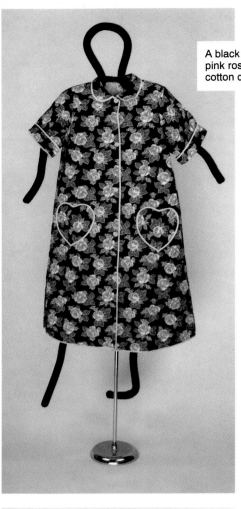

A black background forms a lovely backdrop for the pink roses and piped heart-shaped pockets on this cotton quilted robe by Fruit of the Loom.

Lime green silk bathrobe with applied needlework designs in floral and zig-zag patterns with wrap-around front and attached sash.

Floral printed rayon bathrobe with scalloped collar and cuffs, label reads "Styled by KAMORE."

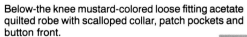

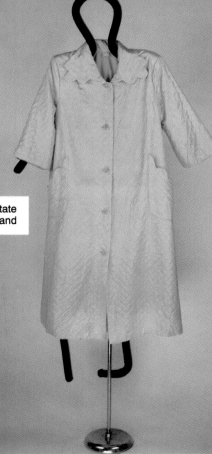

Below-the knee mustard-colored loose fitting acetate quilted robe with scalloped collar, patch pockets and button front.

Lounging robe in floral printed cotton, Spiegel. 1951.

Lounging robe of crinkle cotton in bold leaf print by Sherry Lynn.

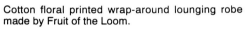

Cotton floral printed wrap-around lounging robe made by Fruit of the Loom.

Quilted lounging robe with lace trim, large side pocket and sash by Evelyn Pearson.

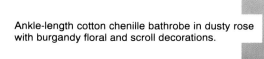

Ankle-length cotton chenille bathrobe in dusty rose with burgandy floral and scroll decorations.

67

Robes for Milady offered for sale in 1951.

Luxurious quilted robe made of mustard-colored acetate with navy blue rayon lining and trim, label reads "Styled by CARO".

Robes always make great Christmas gifts. These examples were offered in 1954 through the Sears Christmas Catalog.

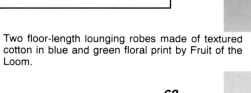

Two floor-length lounging robes made of textured cotton in blue and green floral print by Fruit of the Loom.

Ankle-length tailored bathrobe in cranberry-colored satin quilting with large pocket and sash.

Printed cotton quilted bathrobe with scalloped collar, side pocket and piped trim.

Fruit of the Loom Hi-Style Long Coat Pajama made of Celanese acetate.

Two lovely nightgowns made of rayon in pink and blue pastel with black fan designs printed throughout and nylon lace trim.

Pajamas made of pink rayon with light blue piped trim and mandarin collar, label reads "SKYLON".

Pajamas and pajama sets offered for sale in 1953.

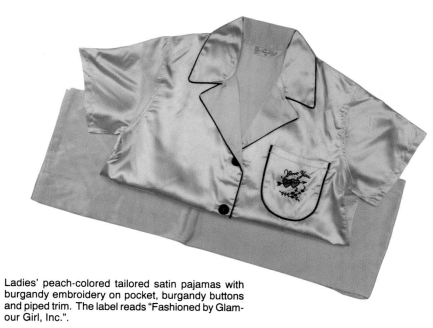

Ladies' peach-colored tailored satin pajamas with burgandy embroidery on pocket, burgandy buttons and piped trim. The label reads "Fashioned by Glamour Girl, Inc.".

Flannel nightgowns have always been a cold weather favorite. These examples were styled for 1958.

Ladies' pajamas and pajama sets made of plisse, flannel, broadcloth and nylon, Montgomery Ward, 1955.

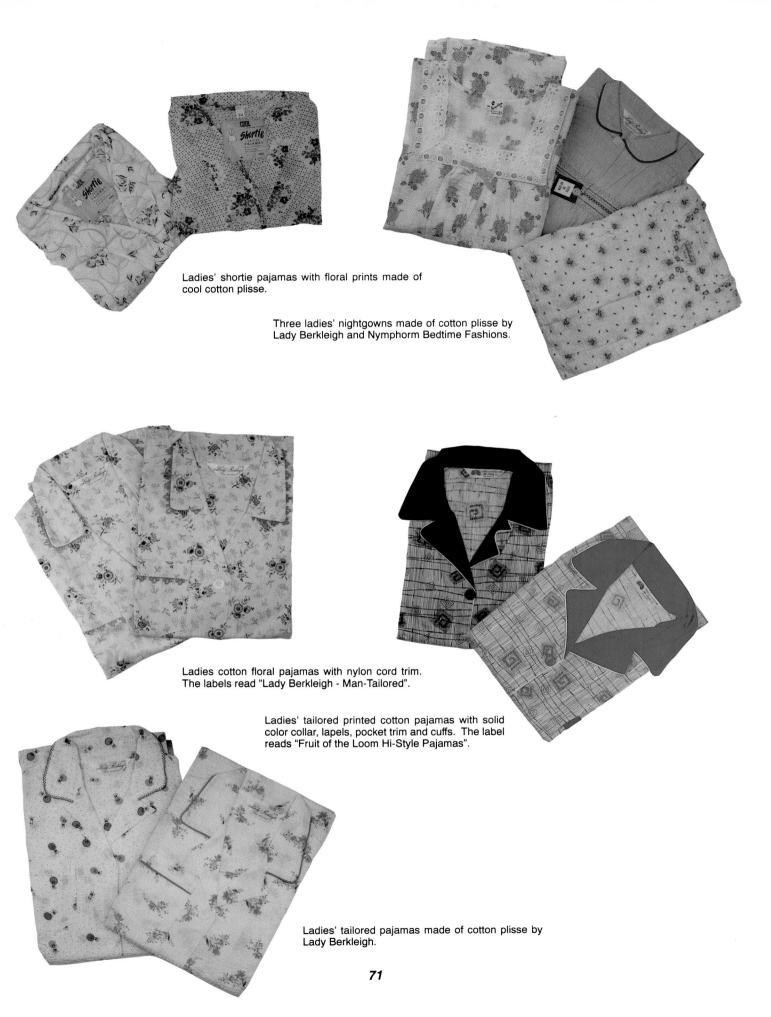

Ladies' shortie pajamas with floral prints made of cool cotton plisse.

Three ladies' nightgowns made of cotton plisse by Lady Berkleigh and Nymphorm Bedtime Fashions.

Ladies cotton floral pajamas with nylon cord trim. The labels read "Lady Berkleigh - Man-Tailored".

Ladies' tailored printed cotton pajamas with solid color collar, lapels, pocket trim and cuffs. The label reads "Fruit of the Loom Hi-Style Pajamas".

Ladies' tailored pajamas made of cotton plisse by Lady Berkleigh.

Due to the lasting popularity of circle skirts throughout the entire decade, petticoats were still extremely fashionable in 1959. These "Flirty Nylon Poufs" were sold through Aldens.

Lacy slips and petticoats offered for sale from National Bellas Hess in 1955.

Saddle shoes made of leather offered for sale in 1951, Sears, Roebuck and Company.

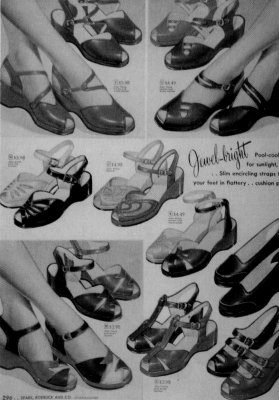

Colorful sandals in leather for the 1951 Spring and Summer season.

Advertised as "Bright Color-Mates for your house-coats," these slippers were offered for sale in 1953.

Casual shoes in colorful leather fashionable in 1953.

Shoes and handbags styled for the 1959 Summer season.

Leather and nylon mesh shoes popular in 1957.

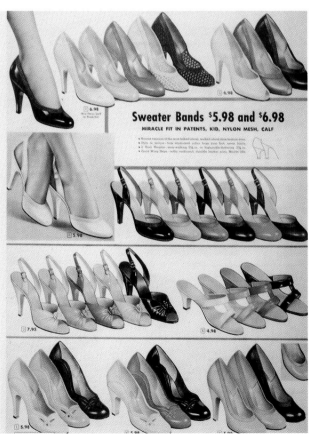

Lovely assortment of high-heeled shoes fashionable in 1953.

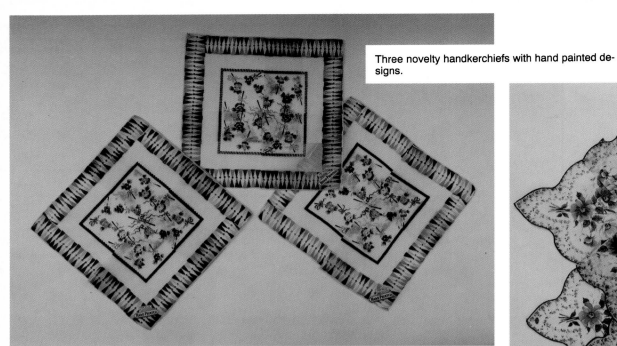

Three novelty handkerchiefs with hand painted designs.

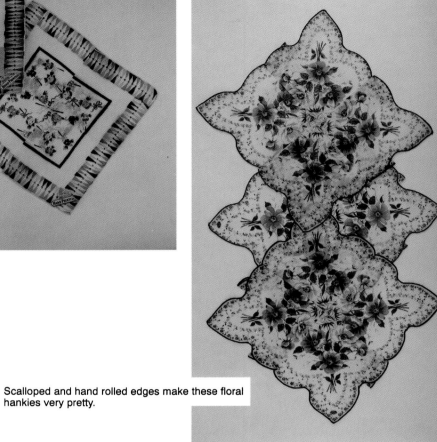

Scalloped and hand rolled edges make these floral hankies very pretty.

Poinsettias and roses were two popular floral themes used in designing handkerchiefs.

Three lovely hankies in shades of lavender with floral themes and a ribbon design that spells "Mother".

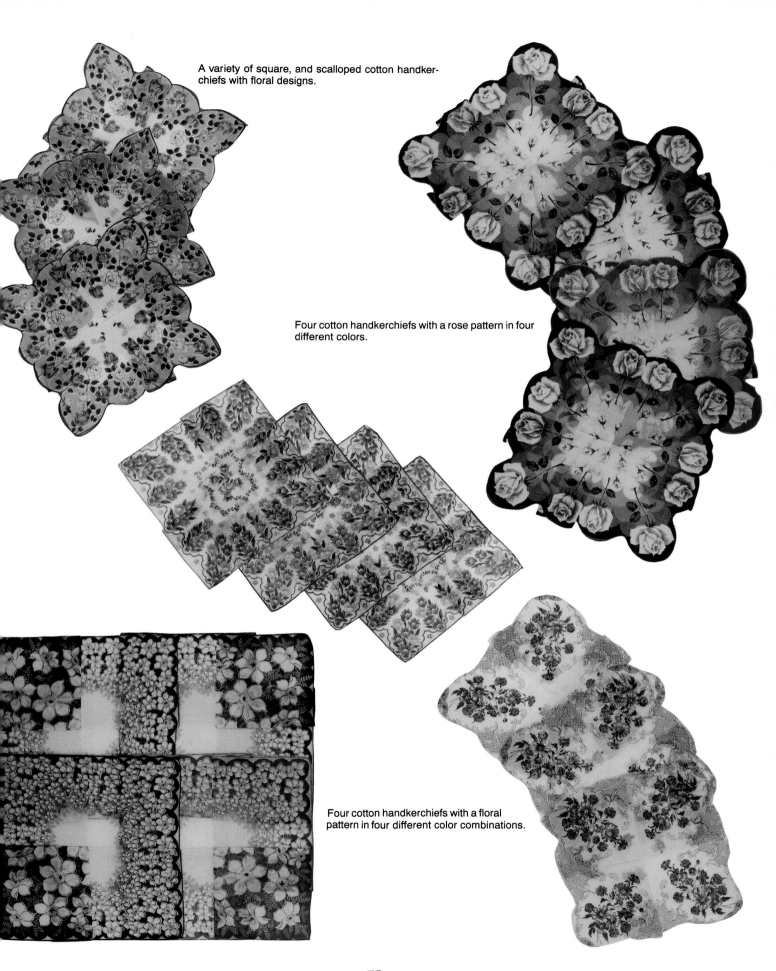

A variety of square, and scalloped cotton handkerchiefs with floral designs.

Four cotton handkerchiefs with a rose pattern in four
different colors.

Four cotton handkerchiefs with a floral
pattern in four different color combinations.

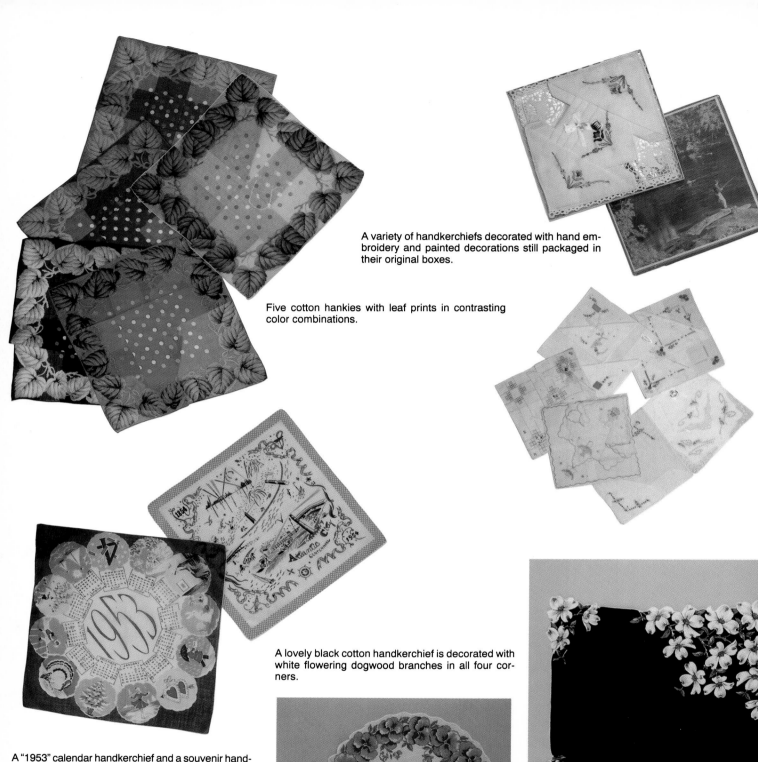

A variety of handkerchiefs decorated with hand embroidery and painted decorations still packaged in their original boxes.

Five cotton hankies with leaf prints in contrasting color combinations.

A "1953" calendar handkerchief and a souvenir handkerchief of the "Atlantic City Centennial" of 1954.

A lovely black cotton handkerchief is decorated with white flowering dogwood branches in all four corners.

Two circular floral cotton handkerchiefs with hand-rolled scalloped edges.

Four sheer nylon scarfs with rhinestone ornamentation and daisy trim.

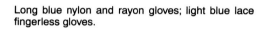

Long blue nylon and rayon gloves; light blue lace fingerless gloves.

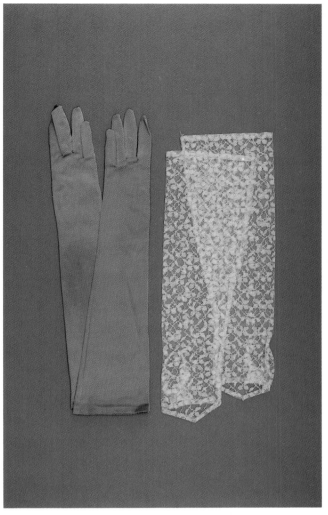

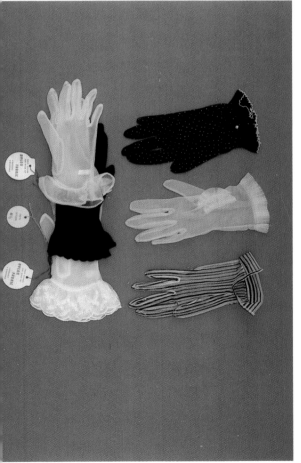

Six pair of gloves made of nylon in solid sheer, striped and flocked designs.

Five pair of gloves made of double woven nylon and cotton.

Spring hats and bonnets for 1955.

Eight hand-made sequined skull caps in a variety of colors worn for evening wear.

Leather pumps, cowhide bag, Italian gloves and sculptured jewelry offered for sale in 1954.

"Dazzling Black Patent" described these accessories in 1957.

Bronze-colored stretch satin gloves made of 40% nylon and 60% rayon and accented with mink trim. They were made in Western Germany.

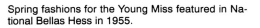

Spring fashions for the Young Miss featured in National Bellas Hess in 1955.

Sweater shrugs for toddlers and little girls were even manufactured in the 1950s made of combed cotton with shell trim by Fame-Tex.

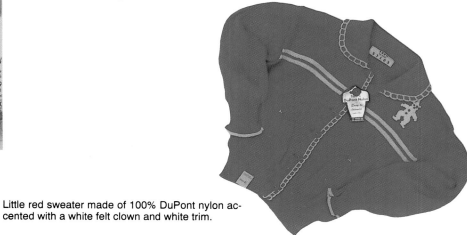

Little red sweater made of 100% DuPont nylon accented with a white felt clown and white trim.

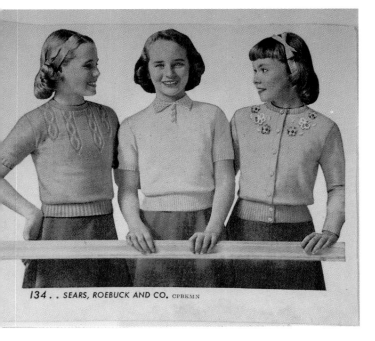

134 . . SEARS, ROEBUCK AND CO. CPBKMN

Pullovers and cardigans made of nylon with "Knit-in designs or trim", Sears, 1955.

Charming button-down cardigan sweaters for girls made of wool and decorated with embroidery. The tags reads "Sterling Children's Wear".

Double-breasted coat and bonnet ensemble made of pink and gray checked rayon gabardine, no label.

Coats for little girls made of rayon, gabardine and wool in a variety of styles and price ranges, Wards, 1953.

Adorable coat and bonnet ensemble made of red wool flannel with detachable plaid taffeta capelet, label reads "Parker Wilder Company, Inc.".

Exquisite coat and hat outfits for little girls offered for sale from Montgomery Ward in 1953.

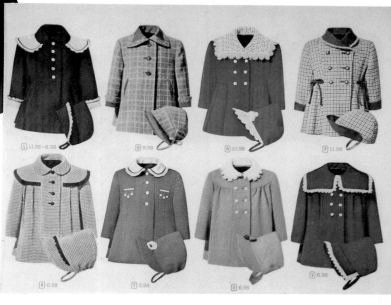

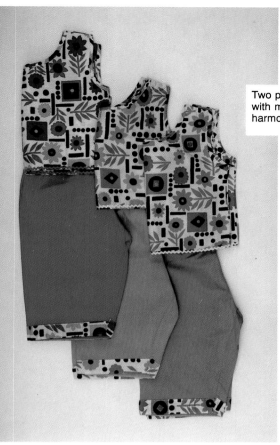

Two piece set for girls consisting of sleeveless top with matching pedal pushers, shown here in three harmonizing color combinations.

Coats with matching bags and Toppers designed for Teens popular in 1953.

Cotton play clothes for girls offered for sale in 1955.

Ensembles and coats for teens fashionable in 1953.

Playwear and dress-up sets for boys and girls for the Summer of 1953.

One piece jumpsuit made of cotton with cinch waist, sailor collar and poodle appliques on pockets.

Medium-weight cotton pedal pushers for girls with plaid trim.

Lightweight cotton pedal pushers for girls in a rainbow of colors with harlequin check trim.

Plaid pullover for girls with ribbed collars and bottoms. The labels read "M.G.M. Margaret O'Brien, Basque shirts Fashioned by Playtown Togs".

Two-piece short set for girls with polka dot sleeveless blouse with solid collar, and solid-color shorts with polka dot trim by Holiday.

Ladies' cotton "Dungarettes" in blue, black and gray by Turner Togs.

Denim jeans for girls with cotton flannel lining, side zipper and button on suspenders by Blue Bell.

Harlequin prints were very common in the 1950s. This two- piece outfit for girls consists of shorts and halter top.

Novelty Western Wear for girls advertised in the Sears catalog in 1951.

Children's robes and slippers offered for sale in 1954.

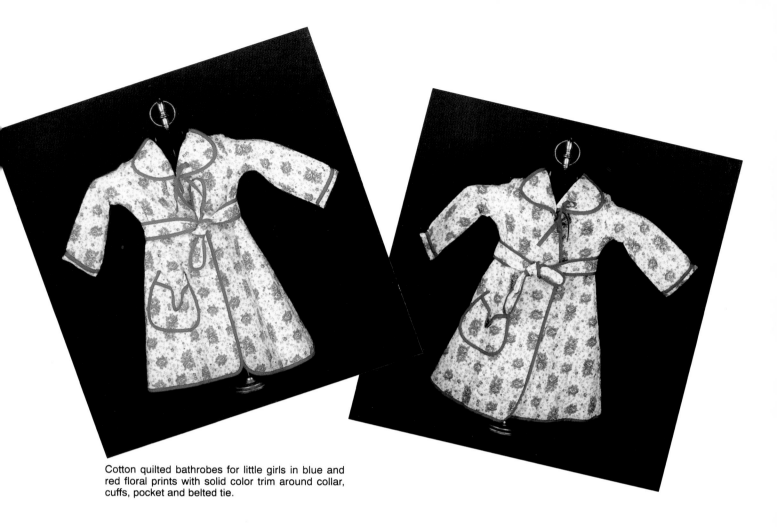

Cotton quilted bathrobes for little girls in blue and red floral prints with solid color trim around collar, cuffs, pocket and belted tie.

Polished cotton play or swim suits for little girls with floral and polka dot designs. The labels read "Blue Bird Knitwear Company".

School books and pencils are printed on these three cotton quilted bathrobes for little girls.

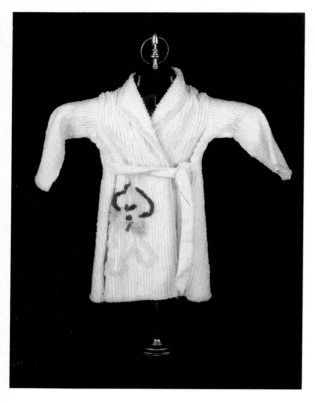

Four cotton chenille bathrobes for little girls in blue, pink, yellow and off-white with puppy dog silhouette by Chenille Tufted Products.

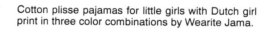

Cotton plisse pajamas for little girls with Dutch girl print in three color combinations by Wearite Jama.

Printed cotton flannel pajamas for girls with nylon lace trim and elastic boxer waist band.

A novelty Indian design was printed on this pair of cotton plisse pajamas.

Cotton pajamas for teens, Sears, 1958.

Novelty pajamas for girls with Indian and guitar prints.

Novelty pajamas for girls made of cotton plisse.

Lingerie for the Young Miss, Sears, 1958.

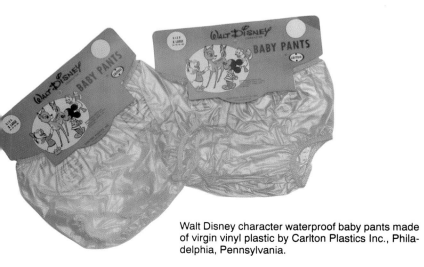

Walt Disney character waterproof baby pants made of virgin vinyl plastic by Carlton Plastics Inc., Philadelphia, Pennsylvania.

Three Cinderella cinch belts for little girls still packaged on their original cards dating from the early 1950s.

More pearl and rhinestone collars that were commonly used to accent dresses, sweaters and suits in the 1950s.

"Oodles of Poodles, Saucy pooches prance on favorite soda crowd separates" described these accessories in 1954.

Four decorative collars made of plain and waffled cotton with lace trim. These collars were extremely fashionable in the 1950s to dress up a simple dress, suit or sweater.

Handmade beaded clutch bag and matching beaded collar decorated with rhinestones and pearls.

Trio of pearl collars that were extremely popular in the 1950s.

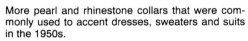

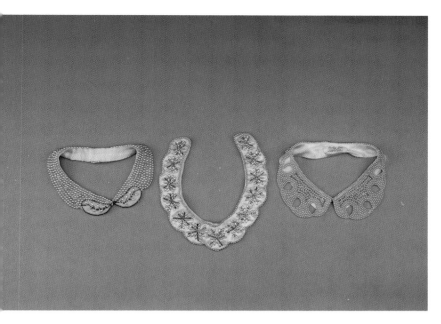

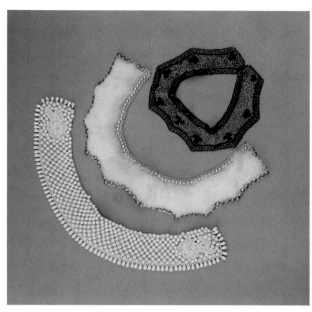

Again pearls and rhinestones were used to fashion these decorative dress accessories.

More collars made of beads, pearls and rabbit fur.

Woolen ski gloves knitted with diamond shapes in multi- colors.

Wool knit gloves decorated with beadwork and embroidery.

Four pair of knit gloves made out of wool decorated with felt puppy dogs.

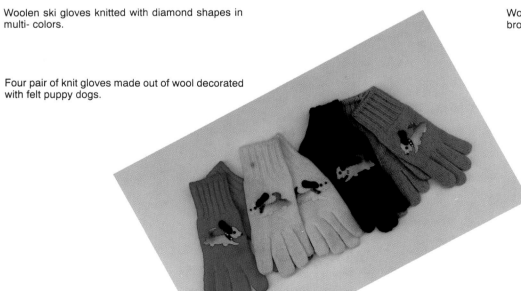

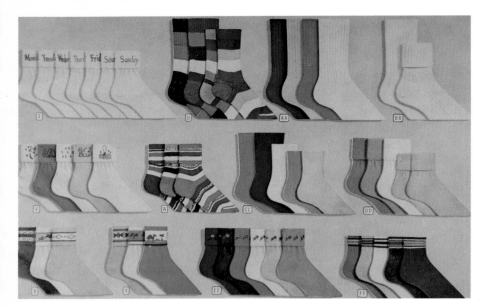

Colorful children's anklets, Wards, 1955.

"Varsity Flip" leather shoes for girls, Aldens, 1959.

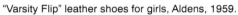

Girl's cotton socks with novelty borders.

Leather dress shoes for girls in strap and pump styles.

Cable knit pullover made of cotton with unusual vertical stripes made by Allen-A Sportswear.

Another cotton cable knit pullover with zig zag horizontal striping by Allen-A Sportswear. The red, white and blue socks were made by Hanes.

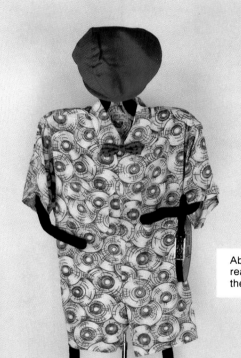

Abstract printed Hawaiian-style rayon shirt, label reads "Lion of Troy". The bow tie is made of silk and the Ivy League cap is made of linen-like rayon.

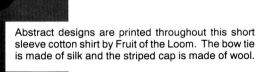

Abstract designs are printed throughout this short sleeve cotton shirt by Fruit of the Loom. The bow tie is made of silk and the striped cap is made of wool.

Stripes and polka dots were used in combination in this cotton shirt by Fruit of the Loom. It looks rather sharp with the white slacks, thin leather belt and wool Ivy League cap.

103

Cotton short sleeve sport shirt with double front pockets and a red, white and black checked pattern by Fruit of the Loom. The yellow and black checked cap is marked "Genuine Woolrich".

Three striped sport shirts for men with button-down collars made by Mark Twain and Fruit of the Loom.

Sport Shirts

With the advent of synthetic "wonder" fabrics after World War II, men's casual clothing changed with respect to durability, range of colors and easier laundering. Tailored gabardine sport shirts with double front pockets and two-way sport collars were available in every color imaginable. In 1953, Sears advertised "Lustrous Rayon Gabardine" sport shirts made of a rayon and acetate blend. The shirts were "...comfortable and easy fitting for casual relaxing wear...yet tailored enough for dressier wear. The long wear and strength of rayon is added to the softness, manageability and fine draping qualities of acetate to make a fine shirt fabric." This particular shirt was available in "eight rich solid hues."

Two paisley print sport shirts for men made of cotton by Fruit of the Loom.

Men's sport shirts made of acetate in brown and green check with short sleeves, double front pockets and wide spread collar by Benham Sportswear.

Other miracle fabrics were blends of Orlon, rayon and acetate which were advertised as "Wash - Drip - Dry and Wear" shirts. Puckered nylon, crinkle crepe, open-weave Leno mesh, cotton poplin, chambray, broadcloth, spun rayon and combed cotton were popular fabrics used for summer shirts. Flannel, corduroy, wool and heavy weight gabardines were popular for winter wear.

Checks, stripes, plaids and foulard patterns in men's Ivy League shirts, Sears, 1958.

Three men's shirts made of cotton with a combination of prints including floral diamond patterns, vertical striping and Trojan helmets. The labels read "Golden Award by Wings".

Two horizontal-striped shirts for men in brown and blue by Fruit of the Loom.

Long sleeve rayon dress shirts for men with embroidered crest designs made by Silver Wings.

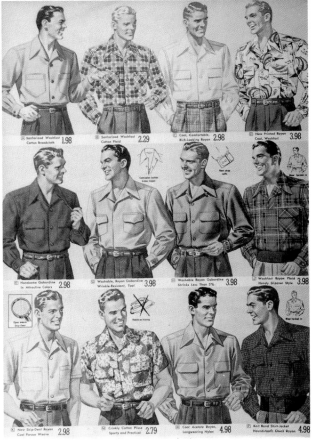

Long and short sleeve sport shirts offered for sale from Spiegel in 1951.

Vertical-striped cotton shirts for men by Fruit of the Loom. Notice the original price of $1.99.

The basic styling of men's shirts remained rather constant throughout the 1950s with the exception of the size of the collar. Also, by this time, button-down collars on shirts were popular, Sears, 1958.

Three shirts for men in rust, brown and iridescent gray rayon by Mark Twain.

Five rayon broadcloth shirts for men with double front pockets and two-way collar by Nelson-Paige.

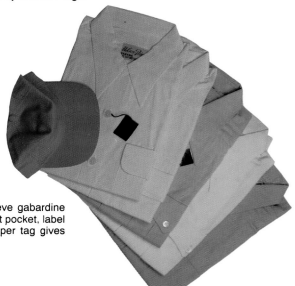

Dark green and navy blue long sleeve gabardine shirts for men designed with one front pocket, label reads "Sportswear". The original paper tag gives detailed washing instructions.

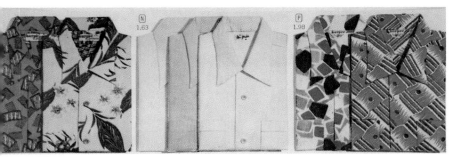

Shirts for men in plain and printed rayon and cotton plisse, Montgomery Ward, 1953.

SPUN RAYON SPORT SHIRTS .. Pre-shrunk to give lasting fit .. "Comfort weight" fabrics for year-around wear $2⁹⁵ Each Any 3 for $8⁵⁵

Dusty blue | Tan | Dusty Gray | Brick red | Kelly green | Maroon | Dark green | Navy

These spun rayon shirts with double front pockets came in a wide variety of colors. The were offered from Sears in 1951.

Casual wear for men offered from Spiegel in 1951. Notice how large and pointed the collars on the shirts were at this time.

This guy is raring to go wearing his dacron and rayon slacks by Lee Tropics, off-white rayon shirt by Nelson-Paige, cowhide belt by Squire and silk floral necktie.

Wrinkle-resistant cotton by Dan River was used to make this gray and burgandy sport shirt styled by Mohawk Sportswear.

Dress Shirts

Dress shirts with button-down collars were seen throughout the decade. Pointed button-down collars were just as popular as those with rounded collars. Popularity increased as the decade progressed and by the late 1950s, casual shirts with printed designs featured button-down collars as well. They were popular with the college kids and sometimes referred to as "Ivy League" shirts. Dacron and Dacron blends were used significantly.

Mr. Debonair is really decked out in this off-white double-breasted gabardine suit, brown rayon shirt by Lion of Troy, brown rayon tie with abstract design, and an off-white small-brimmed hat. Look out Harry Anderson!

Printed cotton shirt with small circular designs made by Town Topic. The green rayon necktie with feather designs has no label, the geometric socks were made by Schofield, and the small-brimmed plaid hat is made of wool.

Fashionable since after World War II, the vogue for Hawaiian shirts lasted well into the 1950s. Rayon was the most common fabric used, although other examples found were made of silk and cotton. Tropical floral and scenic prints in bright and bold color combinations were stylish. Cabana sets consisting of a short sleeve coat-style sport shirt and a pair of swim trunks or shorts were fashionable garments designed for men to wear while vacationing. Tropical prints were often found on these sets.

Gray cotton shirt with horizontal striping in red, black and white was made by Fruit of the Loom. Red waffled rayon necktie with four circular patterns, no label. The gray nylon socks were made by Allen-A Sportswear, and the wool hat has no label.

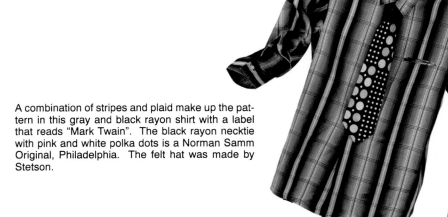

A combination of stripes and plaid make up the pattern in this gray and black rayon shirt with a label that reads "Mark Twain". The black rayon necktie with pink and white polka dots is a Norman Samm Original, Philadelphia. The felt hat was made by Stetson.

Long sleeve gray rayon broadcloth shirt with double flap pockets by Lion of Troy. The green waffled rayon necktie with abstract design has no label. The green geometric socks were made by Schofield and the felt hat was made by Stetson.

Long sleeve tailored shirt made of light blue rayon, label reads "Mohawk". The floral necktie is made of rayon and the blue geometrically-woven nylon socks were made by Schofield.

Bluish-gray rayon shirt with wide spread collar, French cuffs with "Comedy and Tragedy" cuff links and matching buttons, label reads "Mokawk".

Pin-striped shirts for men made of blue and red crinkled cotton, label reads "Terrace Club".

Three "Kool-Weave" nylon sport shirts for men in blue, yellow and green by Terrace Club.

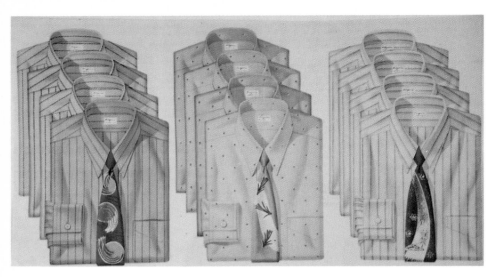

Cotton broadcloth dress shirts for men offered for sale in 1951.

Mustard-colored long sleeve rayon shirt with double button pockets made by Lion of Troy. The brown necktie is also made of rayon and the nylon socks were made by Silver Bond.

Blue cotton shirt with double front pockets and hand stitching on collar and pockets, label reads "Mark Twain". The blue printed rayon necktie has no label and the nylon socks were made by Allen-A Sportswear.

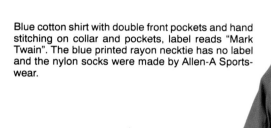

Long sleeve blue and gray dress shirt made of cotton and silk with horizontal banding and vertical striping at yoke, label reads "Elderado". The bow tie is made of silk and the gray cotton cap is marked "Lee".

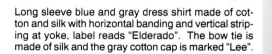

Banded cotton long sleeve shirt, label reads "Elderado Casuals, Porto Fino Cottons, Styled by Di Mercurio". The brown rayon necktie with leaf print has an original tag that reads "Morro Custom Cravats, wrinkle resistant, 100% wool- lined, As advertised in *Esquire*, distributed by Rose Neckwear Company, Philadelphia, Pa.".

Black and gray vertical striped shirt made of cotton by Fruit of the Loom. The Ivy League tweed cap is made of wool.

Casual sport shirt made of cotton, label reads "Leesures by Lee". The wool cap with geometric design has no label.

Coffee with cream is the color of this cotton jacket with black trim, applique and metal buttons by Nortex.

Jackets

The most significant change that occurred with suit and sport jackets was the size of the lapels. After World War II, jackets were designed with wide-peaked lapels, broad padded shoulders and a slightly tapered waist to give the appearance of a taller individual. In the early 1950s, the large lapels were still popular. As the decade progressed, however, the lapels began to get narrower. By 1957, a drastic reduction in the size and the shape of lapels was evidenced.

Casual jackets and shirts featured in the National Bellas Hess catalog in 1955.

MEN'S SPORTSWEAR
JACKETS AND SHIRTS

Part Nylon Gabardine $3.99 UP [A]

Part Nylon Sheen Gabardine $6.99 [B]

Rayon-and-Acetate Gabardine [D] $1.99

100% Nylon

DESCRIPTIONS ON OPPOSITE PAGE

Also Short Sleeves $1.79

Black and white zebra striped jacket made of cotton corduroy with quilted rayon lining by Peters Sportswear Company.

Zippered jacket made of nylon and acetate with quilted rayon lining by Glenhall Sportswear. The fabric was made by Burlington Mills.

Luster twill zipper jacket with fake fur collar and quilted rayon lining by Town Topic.

Men's casual jackets pictured in the Sears Christmas catalog, 1954.

"Hercules Horsehide Jackets" advertised for sale in 1953.

Luster twill jackets for men in Bomber, Motorcycle and Surcoat styles popular in 1953.

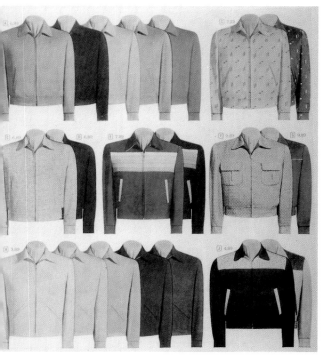

"Sport Denim in 1955's New Colors" made into casual jackets, walking shorts and slacks.

Classic styling and a fine array of colors is displayed in this 1955 jacket offer from Wards.

Trousers

In 1951, men's trousers were fashion tailored with double pleats, a seamless Hollywood waistband and turned-up cuffs. "Conservative Style" trousers had no pleats. In 1953, Montgomery Ward Co. stated that Conservative model slacks were "preferred by thousands of well dressed men." They were "styled with a plain, unpleated front, regular belt loops, suspender buttons and zipper fly." Summer weights, year-round weights and winter weight fabrics were offered. The Conservative model slacks were made to fit lower on the waist than the pleated models and the "California" model fit higher on the waist than the normal pleated version. The California slacks were designed to give the appearance of a "taller, slimmer and more athletic" build. Patterned sharkskin, sheen gabardine, twill gabardine, spun rayon, Orlon and wool were popular fabrics. Tweeds, solids and splash weaves were common. In 1957, slim Ivy League style trousers were becoming fashionable with unpleated fronts and an adjustable rear buckle strap. By 1959, slim trousers were made with side buckles although pleated and conservative styles were still very popular for the well-dressed man.

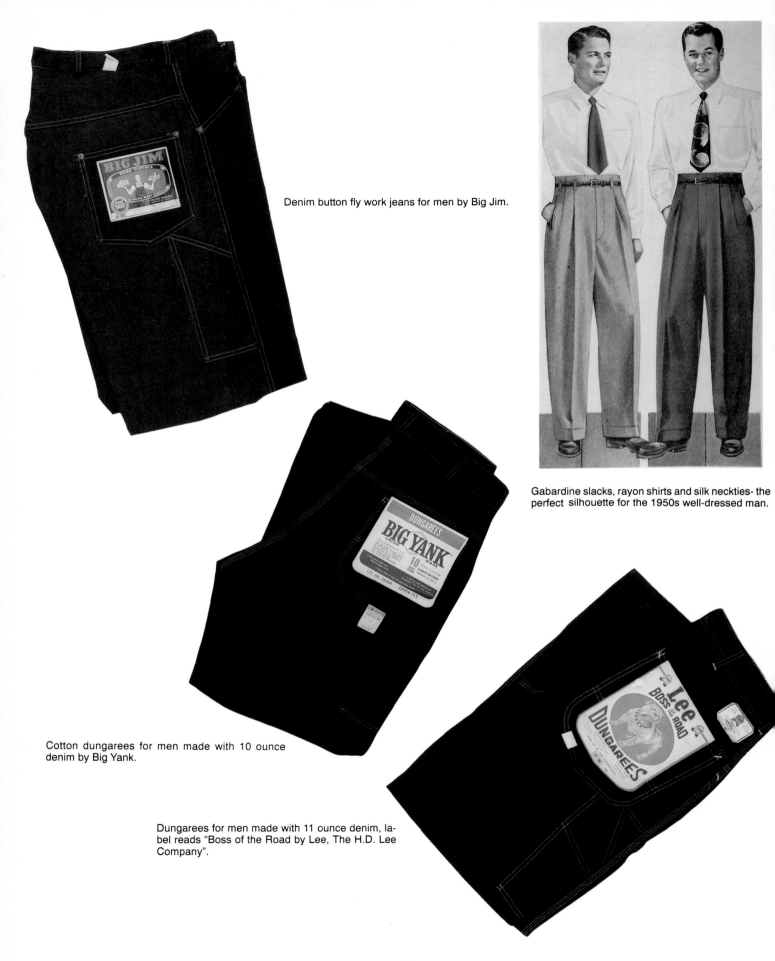

Denim button fly work jeans for men by Big Jim.

Gabardine slacks, rayon shirts and silk neckties- the perfect silhouette for the 1950s well-dressed man.

Cotton dungarees for men made with 10 ounce denim by Big Yank.

Dungarees for men made with 11 ounce denim, label reads "Boss of the Road by Lee, The H.D. Lee Company".

Men's slacks for 1958 made of dacron & wool and orlon & wool.

| 35% DACRON 65% WOOL | 30% ORLON 70% WOOL | 55% DACRON 45% WOOL WORSTED | 50% DACRON 50% WOOL WORSTED |

Suits made of 100% Virgin Wool Worsted Gabardine and offered for sale in 1951.

Mix and match sport clothes in rich color combinations, Montgomery Ward, 1953.

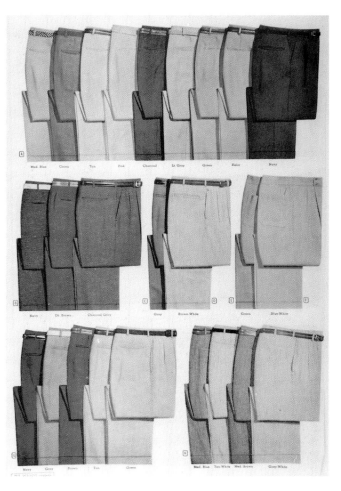

"Men's Warm-weather slacks" made of: (a) Dacron blend or gabardine, (b) rayon, (c) Army twill, (d) combed cotton, (e) rayon, (f) cotton & rayon, (g) Dacron and (h) Orlon & nylon, Wards, 1955.

Men's Leisure Jackets made of rayon gabardine and pinwale corduroy offered for the 1954 Christmas Season.

Men's slacks in fashionable tweeds, flannels, splash weaves and gabardine, Sears, 1954.

B or C
SPORT COATS
$22⁵⁰

B or C
SLACKS
$10⁴⁰

SAVE $1.15 on 2-PC. OUTFIT
$31⁷⁵
Cash
$3.50 Down

Fashion Tailored
100% VIRGIN WOOL
year 'round SPORT COATS
with 100% WOOL WORSTED
4-Star Feature SLACKS

All Coats and Slacks Described
on Facing Page

Wool Sport coats and slacks fashionable in 1955.

"Executive, Diplomat and Cosmopolitan" were the names used to describe these suits made in 1951.

Blue striped satin lounging robe with navy blue satin lining, lapels, cuffs and belted sash. The label reads "State-O- Maine".

Robes

Classic lounge wear for men has become quite collectible. Long robes or shorter smoking jackets made of rayon and rayon jacquard were expertly tailored in the late 1940s and 1950s. Fine robes made with beautiful jacquard weaves were designed with contrasting satin trim and full satin linings. Many other fabrics were popular for robe manufacture including flannel, gabardine, terry cloth, puckered nylon and cotton plisse. Lightweight acetates were used to manufacture robes that could be folded very small and put into a matching zippered pouch. These robes were advertised as perfect for traveling. Paisleys, plaids, foulards, stripes, jacquards and solids were popular. One of the longest wearing robe fabrics was Beacon cloth made of Estron acetate and cotton. Beacon robes were made for men and boys alike. The Ombre pattern, which was a shaded design on a solid background, was the most popular.

Smoking jackets, also called TV jackets, were extremely fashionable for men in the 1950s. This example, made of silver-colored rayon with black satin trim has a label that reads "His Excellency Designer Collection".

A gentleman's lounging robe of navy blue rayon with polka dot collar, cuffs, pocket flaps and sash. The label reads "Elite".

Printed lounging robe made of rayon by "Hego". Label also reads "Planned fabric of rayon containing Celanese yarn."

Robes for men made of flannel, gabardine and terry cloth, Sears, 1954.

Another lounging robe made of burgandy rayon with polka dot trim by "Elite".

Black and gold Oriental lounging robe and matching slippers (in pocket) with gold cord belt made in Korea.

Red smoking jacket with paisley print and black collar, cuffs and belted tie, label reads "Overkirk".

Burgundy rayon and satin lounging robe made by "Elite".

Jacquard lounging robes and shorter TV jackets offered for sale in 1954.

Nightwear for men in solids, stripes and prints made of cotton broadcloth, crinkle crepe and nylon puckerette, Wards, 1953.

Lounging pajamas made of broadcloth and flannel in checks, plaids and prints, Sears, 1954.

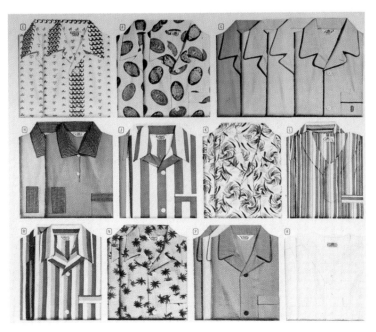

Men's pajamas offered for sale in 1955.

119

Three acetate neckties with small prints designed by Morro.

Three neckties in brown and beige tones made of silk and rayon. The brown silk tie with leaf designs is signed Schiaparelli.

Three rayon neckties with different circle designs by Morro.

Neckties

Another facet of collectible menswear are vintage neckties. Viewed by many as "wearable art," these colorful gems were made in the 1940s and early 1950s. Wide ties made of rayon, rayon jacquard, silk, nylon crepe and acetate were decorated with big and bold designs in bright color combinations. Designs ranged from abstract, geometric, surrealistic and three-dimensional to those depicting flowers, leaves, fish, birds, horses and dogs. Western motifs were common as well as those featuring sailboats, musical instruments, cars, palm trees, naked women and exotic dancers. Neckties were also monogrammed or personalized. The designs found on most of the vintage neckwear from this period were printed onto the fabric. Hand-painted neckties were also plentiful at that time.

Rayon and silk neckties with western, figural and leaf designs. The center example, made of silk is marked "Countess Wara, New York".

Three neckties fashioned from acetate and rayon jacquard by Morro and Durabilt.

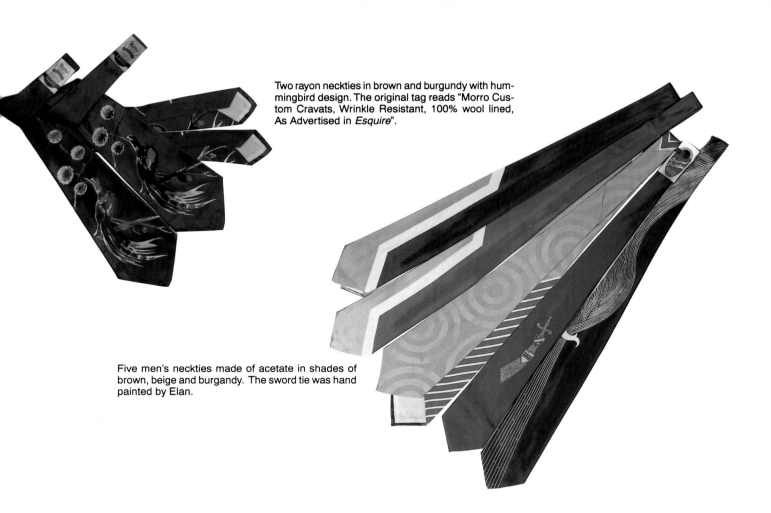

Two rayon neckties in brown and burgundy with hummingbird design. The original tag reads "Morro Custom Cravats, Wrinkle Resistant, 100% wool lined, As Advertised in *Esquire*".

Five men's neckties made of acetate in shades of brown, beige and burgandy. The sword tie was hand painted by Elan.

Eight boy's neckties made of rayon and acetate with geometric designs.

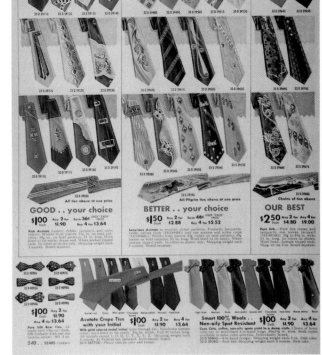

Assortment of bow ties and neckties made of silk, wool and acetate in a variety of prints popular in 1953.

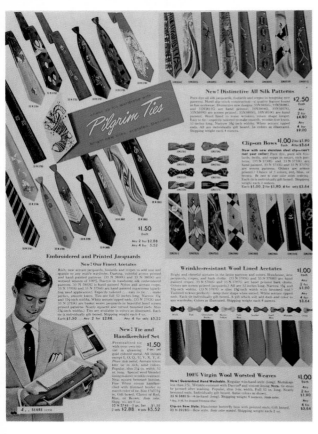

Notice in this 1958 advertisement how men's neckties became dramatically thinner than their counterparts in the early part of the decade.

Latest Fashion Neckwear for style-minded men

The perfect gift for a man - these bright colored beauties were offered for sale in 1954 in the Sears Christmas Catalog.

Men's socks by Silver Bond made of cotton and rayon.

The very same designs are seen here in five different color combinations. These nylon socks were made by Schofield.

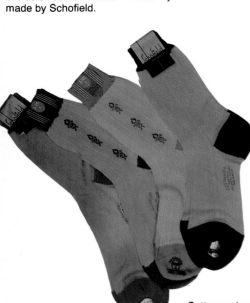

Four pair of men's socks in blue, gray, green and brown nylon with geometric designs by Schofield.

Cotton and rayon socks for men in pastel shades by Schofield and Allen-A Sportswear.

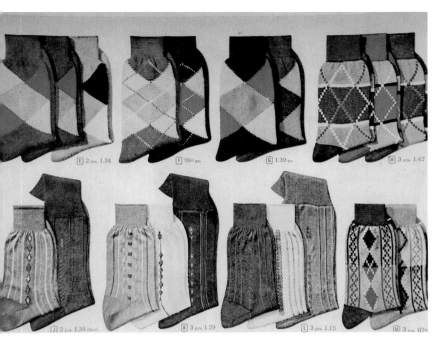

Cotton and nylon socks for men in colorful patterns,
Montgomery Ward, 1953.

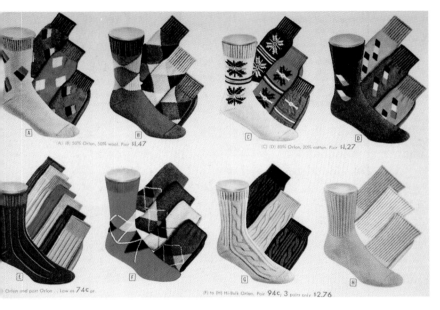

Men's socks made of Orlon and Orlon blends, Sears,
1958.

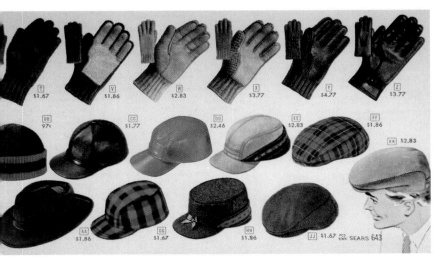

Popular styles in men's socks for 1951.

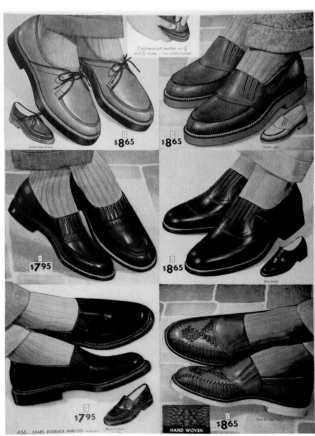

Leather shoes for men offered for sale in 1955.

Gloves and caps for men styled for sport and casual
wear, Sears, 1954.

Great looking shoes for men offered for sale in 1955.

Fur felt, water repellent and Imported Panama hats offered for sale in 1953.

Six pair of nylon stretch socks for men with argyle, checked and abstract patterns.

Men's leather belts still packaged in original presentation boxes made by Squire.

A gift ensemble for a man consisting of stretch nylon socks, custom-made necktie, hand-painted wooden tie rack and fully automatic Ronson cigarette lighter.

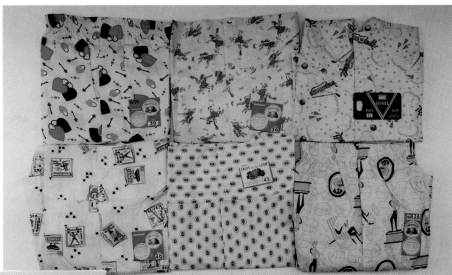

Men's boxer shorts by Fruit of the Loom. Check out some of these prints...hearts, golf clubs, muscle men and cave men. What imagination.

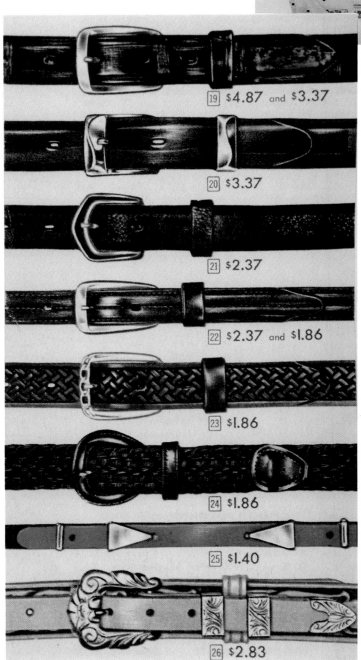

19 $4.87 and $3.37

20 $3.37

21 $2.37

22 $2.37 and $1.86

23 $1.86

24 $1.86

25 $1.40

26 $2.83

Popular styles in men's leather belts for 1954.

Boy's jackets in fashionable Luster Twill and cotton
poplin advertised for sale in 1953.

Two-piece outfit for Junior boys made of sport denim in blue and gray with ribbed collar, cuffs and bottom. Label reads "Tom Sawyer, Jackets for Real Boys". The original tag reads "Elder Manufacturing Co., St. Louis. Mo.".

Chapter IV
Fashions for Young Men and Boys

Just as teenage girls were influenced by Rock & Roll and Hollywood film stars, teenage boys were inspired by Elvis Presley, Marlon Brando and James Dean. Originally designed and worn as work pants, denim blue jeans were worn with tee shirts and leather jackets. Changes in attitudes were reflected in rapid changing dress styles. Jeans were also styled for young boys and toddlers, advertised as "rugged play clothes." Often, they were lined with cotton flannel in bright-colored plaids. Ivy League style clothing was also popular for male college students. Casual sport shirts with button-down collars, cardigan sweaters, trousers with tapered legs and Oxford shoes were fashionable in the late 1950s.

Athletic-style reversible jackets made of wool and acetate satin offered for sale in 1955.

DOUBLE-DUTY REVERSIBLE JACKETS

"Athletic" style 2-in-1 reversible jacket for **$6.98** boys 8 to 18. One side of 100% reprocessed wool melton; opposite side of water-repellent treated lustrous acetate-satin. Practical snap-fastener front, colorful double braid trimming on sleeves; 2 roomy reinforced slash pockets on each side. Contrasting striped knit collar, cuffs and bottom keep body warmth sealed in. Order letter at left.
  State size 8, 10, 12, 14, 16, 18. See chart left. Shpg. wt. 2 lbs. 12 oz.
40 K 6670—Navy-blue and gold
40 K 6671—Maroon combination
40 K 6673—Green and gold...**$6.98**

POPULAR REVERSIBLE JACKET **$4.98** at an unusually low price. One side of lustrous acetate-satin with opposite side of harmonizing cotton poplin. Both sides water-repellent. Snap front; double-braid trim; 2 slash pockets. Knit collar, cuffs and bottom trap body warmth.
  State size 8, 10, 12, 14, 16, 18. See size chart left. Shipping wt. 1 lb. 11 oz.
40 K 3417—Scarlet   **40 K 3419**—Green
40 K 3415—Black   **40 K 3416**—Royal blue
Each.. ....**$4.98**

PCBKMN **PAGE 335 .. BOYS' JACKETS**

A blend of wool, cotton and rayon was used to create this button-down cardigan sweater with knitted bird design. The label reads "Schofield Products Sportswear".

Royal blue and dark green Ivy League wool sweaters trimmed in white. The label reads "Ronny-Lee Sportswear, by S. Segal & Son".

Advertised as "New Styles, New Colors in Jackets for All Boys", these zippered-jackets were made of cotton poplin, rayon acetate and sheen gabardine, Wards, 1955.

Wool and cotton sweaters for boys in pullover, turtle neck and cardigan styles, Sears, 1953.

Boy's slack sets made of rayon in popular 1950s color combinations by Play Pals. The painted trim on the shirts was done by Ventex Finishing Corporation, Paterson, New Jersey.

Cotton flannel shirt for Junior boys with cross stripes in blue, black, beige and gray, accented with corduroy collar. The label reads "Tom Sawyer, Guaranteed Completely".

An illusion of a shirt and a vest was created in the exclusive design of these one-piece garments by Tom Sawyer.

Boy's cotton flannel shirt with reindeer design, label reads "Jibs".

Tri-color cotton shirt for boys with two-way sports collar, ribbed cuffs and bottom by Jets. Notice the similarities in the clothes that were designed for boys. In most instances, they were almost exact copies of those designed for men.

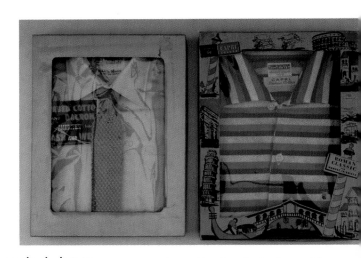

Dress Shirts

Throughout the period, however, whatever was designed for men was also similarly designed for young men and boys. Pleated pants were offered as well as dress shirts with spread collars and French cuffs. Shirts came packaged with a pair of jeweled or gold tone cuff links and sometimes a bow tie or necktie to match. Neckwear for boys was styled almost exactly like men's neckwear. New color combinations such as pink and gray or turquoise and black were also seen in fashions for young men and boys, especially shirts and zippered jackets. Knit pullovers with hand-screened prints were popular as well as sport shirts with novelty checks, plaids, stripes and heraldics. Marine, Mexican and tropical motifs were seen throughout the decade. Gabardine, puckered nylon, cotton plisse, rayon and broadcloth were used.

Boy's white dress shirt of combed cotton and dacron with knit tie by Kaynee in original box. Striped sport shirt with Capri Italian collar by Tom Sawyer, also in original box.

Novelty pullovers for Junior boys and men in jacquard knit or hand-screened prints, Sears, 1951.

130

Cotton flannel and pinwale corduroy shirts for Junior boys advertised for sale in 1953.

Fraternity Prep sport shirts in five colors with decorative hand stitching, Sears, 1955.

Genuine zipper fly denim cowboy pants for boys with red and black checked flannel lining. The original tag reads "Lee Riders Cowboy Pants, circa1946".

Western

American collectors have become pre-occupied with the Old West. Today, everything Western from saddles and spurs to make-believe cowboy and cowgirl outfits from the 1950s are sought after. Children who grew up in the 1950s were inspired by Roy Rogers, Dale Evans and Hopalong Cassidy. Television Westerns provided the impetus for imagination and manufacturers brought the make-believe to life. Complete outfits were designed and manufactured for the little buckaroo. Toy guns, holsters, badges, watches, belts, books, lunch boxes and many other types of Western gear were produced. Mail order companies offered Western outfits for boys and girls. Sears Roebuck & Co. specialized in authentic Roy Rogers and Dale Evans outfits and accessories and the Christmas catalog books were loaded with merchandise that every boy and girl dreamed about owning.

Linen-like rayon sport shirt in beige and rust with two-way sports collar and ribbed bottom. The label in this shirt reads "Soap 'n' Water Fabric, Unconditionally washable, Crown Fabrics, New York".

Novelty shirts for boys were very common in the 1950s. These three examples made of polished cotton are accented with dark collars and closures for wooden shank buttons. They were made by Tom Sawyer.

Summer sport shirts made of cotton in plaid designs accented with wooden buttons by Tom Sawyer. The original paper tag reads "Elder Manufacturing Company, St. Louis".

Western print shirt made of cotton with wagon train theme, label reads "Delsea Jr. Sportswear".

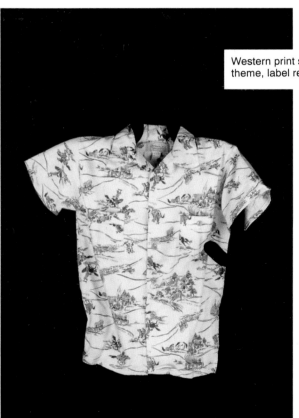

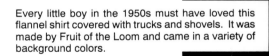

Every little boy in the 1950s must have loved this flannel shirt covered with trucks and shovels. It was made by Fruit of the Loom and came in a variety of background colors.

Combed cotton pullover shirts for men by Allen-A Sportswear.

Combed cotton knit pullover shirts for boys in black/pink and yellow/black color combinations by Tom Sawyer.

Boy's cotton flannel shirt with floral print, label reads "Big League". This particular shirt is a size 16.

Shirts for boys in novelty, western and casual styles, Spiegel, 1951.

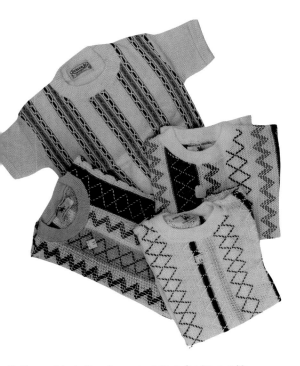

Cotton cable knit pullover sweaters for boys with colorful geometric designs by Schofield and Delsea.

Three knit pullover shirts for boys made with cotton yarn by Kaynee.

Boy's dress shirts in gray, blue and brown cotton with silver satin striping. The labels read "Crest of Quality, Kaynee, Wash n' Wear, Cotton & Cupioni".

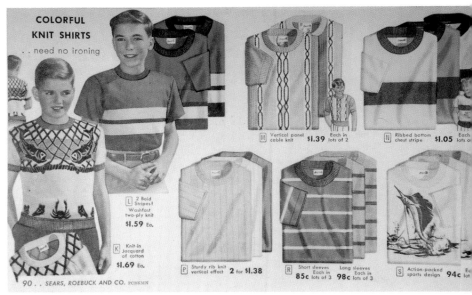

Knit shirts for boys were fashionable throughout the 1950s. These examples were offered for sale in 1951.

Slack sets for boys consisting of solid-color rayon cuffed pants with striped cotton shirts by Little Ruffy Togs.

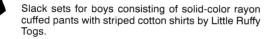

Boy's dress shirts with cross stripes made of rayon by Tom Sawyer.

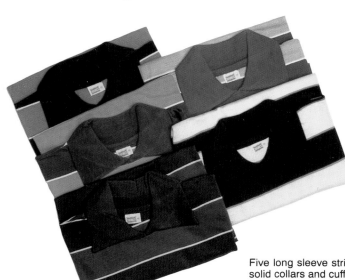

Five long sleeve striped cotton pullover shirts with solid collars and cuffs made by Hanes.

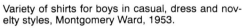

Variety of shirts for boys in casual, dress and novelty styles, Montgomery Ward, 1953.

Rayon and cotton shirts for boys and Junior boys in novelty prints, solids, stripes and dress styles, Wards, 1955.

Three cotton broadcloth shirts for boys with splash check print made by Town Topic.

Three pair of pajamas for boys made of cotton plisse and cotton broadcloth by Sure Rest, Town Topic and Sanford.

Multi-colored plaid short sleeve sport shirts for boys with black and white knit collar by Tom Sawyer. The original tag reads "New with Duratex Fab Gets Wash Clean Clear Thru and Deodorized, too!....and wonderful for dishes. Colgate- Palmolive Company, New York, New York".

Three multi-colored printed cotton shirts with button-down collars by Tom Sawyer.

Two boy's shirts made of flannel with unusual vertical striping and solid color collars and pocket flaps. The label reads "Tom Sawyer, Exclusive Design".

Two identical cotton flannel shirts for boys in blue and red with reindeer print by Jibs.

G Heavier Sanforized, bright cotton flannel $1.45 Ea. in lots of 3

H Heavier Sanforized, woven cotton flannel $1.45 Ea. in lots of 3

J Our heaviest, warmest Sanforized, washfast cotton flannel $1.79

K Heavier Sanforized western plaid 'n' plain cotton flannel $1.97

L Heavy Sanforized, washfast cotton flannel $1.29 Ea. in lots of 2

M New SPACE PATTERN shirt of Sanforized, washfast flannel $1.79

Boy's cotton flannel shirts in plaids, checks and prints, Sears, 1953.

Long sleeve gabardine shirts for boys with double front pockets made just like Dads' by Fruit of the Loom.

Five shirts for boys made of sheer puckered nylon by DuPont.

Three cotton sport shirts fashioned with a diagonal check by Tommy Tucker.

Three summer sport shirts for boys with abstract patterns in three color combinations by Jets.

Four dress shirts for boys in blue, gray, white and beige rayon with satin trim by Tom Sawyer.

Five short sleeve sport shirts for boys fashioned in a rainbow of colors by Jets.

Five summer sport shirts for boys made of textured nylon with novelty and abstract prints. The labels read "100% DuPont Nylon".

Multi-colored plaid flannel shirts for boys by Tom Sawyer.

Plaid cotton flannel shirts for Junior boys by Town Topic.

Heavy-weight western style flannel shirts for boys by Jibs.

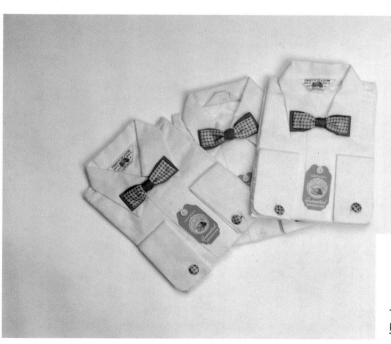

Cotton flannel shirts for boys in different plaids and checks made by Fruit of the Loom.

These white dress shirts with French cuffs came packaged with the bow ties and matching cuff links. They were made by Fruit of the Loom.

Boy's dress shirts accented with glass cuff links by Tom Sawyer.

Casual suits and sport coats for boys fashionable in 1953.

Three long sleeve cotton dress shirts for boys packaged with matching bow ties and cuff links by Tom Sawyer.

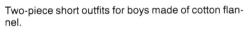

Two-piece short outfits for boys made of cotton flannel.

Two boy's gabardine sport shirts with saddle stitched collar and pockets, in two different shades of pink, both by Tom Sawyer.

Two-piece cotton slacks outfit for boys with plaid shirts and solid-color pants by Tommy Tucker.

Dress-up clothes for young boys in the popular pinks and grays, Wards, 1955.

Three coordinated short sets for boys in popular 1950s color combinations by Tommy Tucker.

FLANNEL LINED

8-oz. Denim Jeans, Jacket, Cap Matching cotton flannel shirt

Suspender Jeans $2.39
Shirt $1.77

Denim Jacket $2.39
Cap $1.19

6-oz. Boxer Jeans $1.79

90 .. SEARS CPBKMN

Play, casual, novelty and dress fashions for young boys popular in 1951.

Flannel-lined denim play clothes for boys advertised for sale in 1953.

Dress-Up sets for little boys made of linen-like rayon, cotton broadcloth and rayon gabardine, Wards, 1955.

Knit pullovers for little boys with skaters, rodeo champs and football players, label reads Andover. (Rodeo champ shirt featured on page 152.)

Short sets for boys with nautical prints in blue, yellow and red crinkled cotton.

Two piece shorts outfit for boys made of cotton plisse with Mexican sombrero print by Tommy Tucker. Two different color combinations are shown here.

Boy's knitted pullover made of combed cotton with "All American" football motif by Andover.

Knitted cardigan sweaters for boys, made of wool and Orlon, with geometric designs by Blue Bird and Havenshire Knitwear Company.

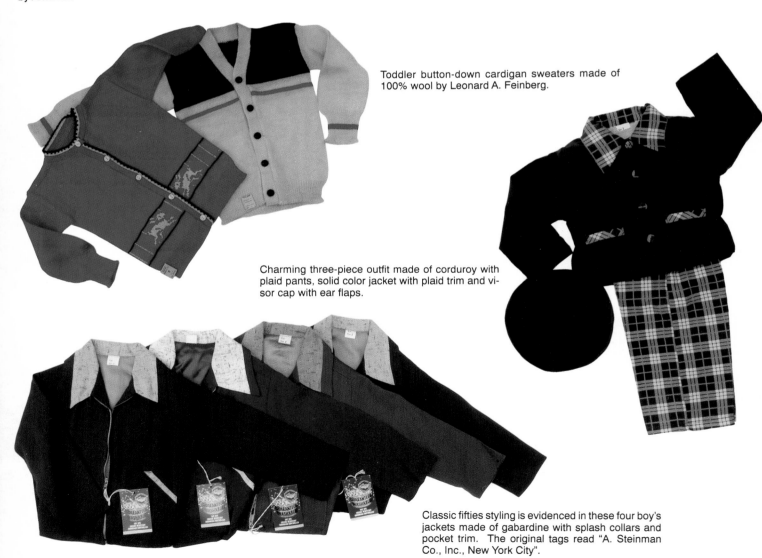

Toddler button-down cardigan sweaters made of 100% wool by Leonard A. Feinberg.

Charming three-piece outfit made of corduroy with plaid pants, solid color jacket with plaid trim and visor cap with ear flaps.

Classic fifties styling is evidenced in these four boy's jackets made of gabardine with splash collars and pocket trim. The original tags read "A. Steinman Co., Inc., New York City".

142

A geometric snowflake pattern was knitted into this wool button-down cardigan sweater for Junior boys.

Three-piece water repellent snowsuit in royal blue and gray rayon and wool. The label reads "Styled by Gloria, Kiddie Togs Corporation".

Boy's pullover sweater made of wool with skier and snowflake pattern. The label reads "Packard Knitwear Co., Philadelphia, Pa.".

Two-piece outfit with two-toned zippered jacket accented with western embroidery and solid-color jodhpurs. The label in this outfit reads "Playland Sportswear, New York".

Outdoor suits for young boys made of wool tweed, wool and nylon plaid and luster twill, Sears, 1953.

Striped pajamas for boys made of crinkle cotton. The original band wrapper reads "For comfort and fit, insist on Child's-Health, Creator of Patented Krotch Pajama, Guaranteed to give satisfaction".

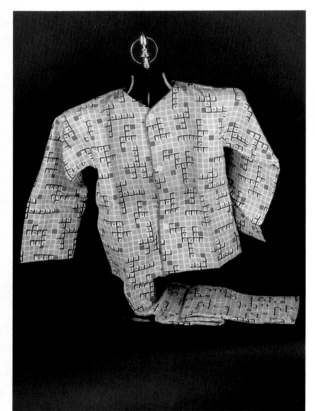

Caps for boys made of wool, nylon and capeskin in popular styles for 1953.

Cotton flannel novelty pajamas with scrabble game print, label reads "Wearite Jama".

Boy's leisure suits in brown and blue gabardine with checked trim. The original tag reads "Four-Square, Sharp Brothers".

Trio of beacon cloth robes for boys with piped trim and cord belts, no label.

A geometric pattern is displayed on this beacon cloth robe for boys with silk cord tie, no label.

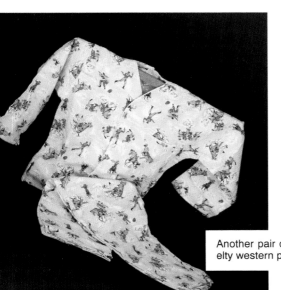

Three novelty knitted baseball pullovers made of combed cotton by Allen-A Sportswear.

Another pair of cotton flannel pajamas with a novelty western print.

D Roy Rogers Robe of Cotton Beacon Cloth $3.98

G Warm flannel Robe of 75% wool and 25% rayon $4.29

M Colorful plaid Robe of Cotton blanket cloth $3.39

JR. BOYS ROBES

Robes for Junior boys made of Beacon cloth, flannel and cotton, Sears, 1953.

Cotton pajamas for boys in prints, stripes and solids, Sears, 1953.

Bow ties made of printed rayon by Cardinal and Ambassador.

Silk and rayon bow ties in a wide variety of styles and designs for both men and boys.

Neckties for boys were style just like those made for men. These five examples were made of rayon and fashioned by Oxford and Varsity.

Eight bow ties made of rayon on original display card which reads, "Just Like Dad's". Notice the original selling price of 39 cents!

Novelty socks for children with nursery rhyme themes.

Boy's argyle socks of soft spun cotton.

Variety of socks for men and boys by Schofield, Hanes, and J.W. Landerberger Co., Philadelphia, Pennsylvania.

Boy's socks in multi-colored striped patterns.

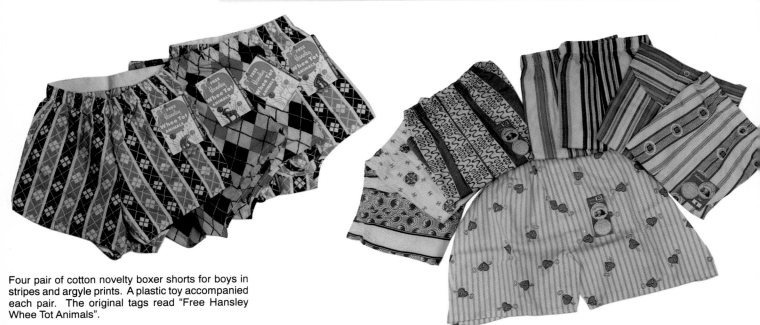

Four pair of cotton novelty boxer shorts for boys in stripes and argyle prints. A plastic toy accompanied each pair. The original tags read "Free Hansley Whee Tot Animals".

Printed boxer shorts for boys by Fruit of the Loom.

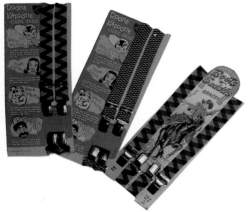

Novelty suspenders for boys on original presentation cards which read "Rootie Kazootie" and "Boots 'n' Saddles".

Combed cotton argyle socks for boys in three color combinations.

148

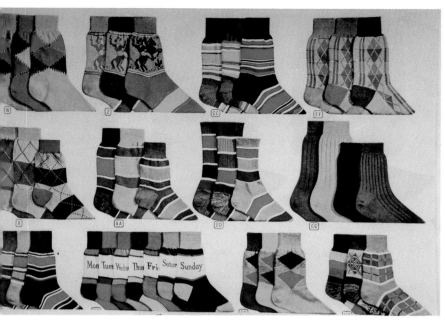

Socks for boys popular in 1953 in diamond argyle, stripes, solids and novelty prints.

Six pair of gloves and mittens made out of cloth and vinyl with novelty ornamentation.

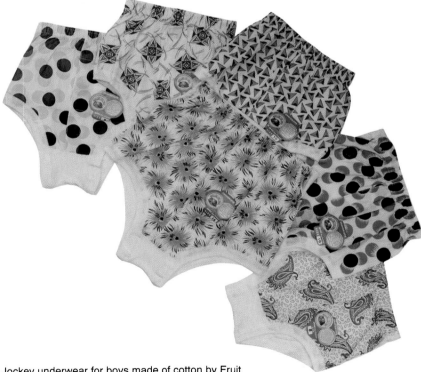

Jockey underwear for boys made of cotton by Fruit of the Loom. Prints were so popular in the 1950s that manufacturers utilized them even in undergarments.

Western style red plaid flannel shirt with yellow piped trim, label reads "Buffalo Bill".

Two-toned cotton western-style shirt with multi-colored scroll embroidery at yoke. Label reads "Jets, Inc.".

Two western style shirts, two-toned in color, accented with brass studs, piping and embroidery, label reads "Jets Inc.".

Roy Rogers and Dale Evans western outfits advertised in the 1954 Sears Christmas Catalog.

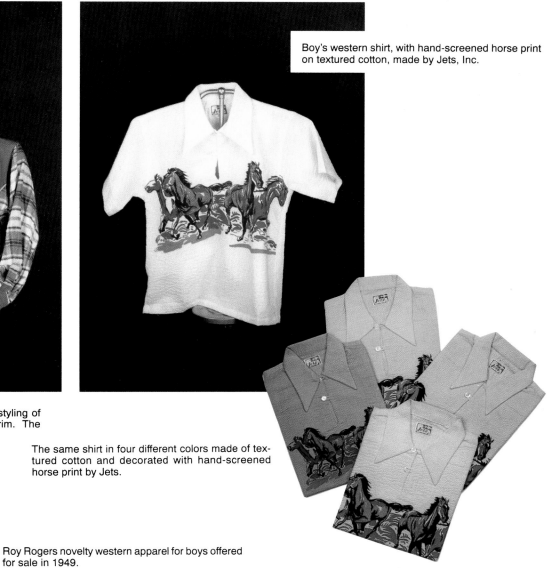

Boy's western shirt, with hand-screened horse print on textured cotton, made by Jets, Inc.

Boy's shirt made of flannel with western styling of plaid design, solid-color yoke and piped trim. The label in this shirt reads "Buffalo Bill".

The same shirt in four different colors made of textured cotton and decorated with hand-screened horse print by Jets.

Roy Rogers novelty western apparel for boys offered for sale in 1949.

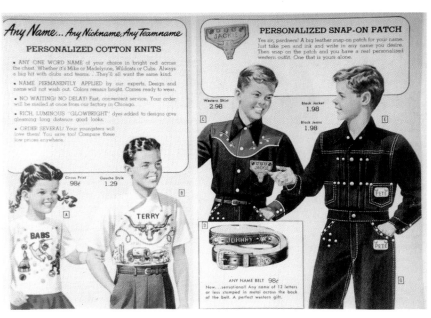

Personalized clothing for boys and girls fashionable in 1951 and offered from Spiegel.

Play and dress clothes for boys and girls, Sears, 1954.

Button-down cardigan sweater for boys, made of wool, knitted with Indian, totem pole and tepee designs. The label reads "Ronny-Lee Sportswear by S. Segal & Son".

Boy's jodhpurs with button-on suspenders, yellow piping and embroidered horse designs on both pockets.

Four western-style Bobby Benson shirts decorated with painting and embroidery, labels read "Sportswear for Better Trade".

Boy's western-style shirt, painted and embroidered with the name, Bobby Benson. The label reads "Sportswear for Better Trade".

Two different Bat Masterson costumes copyrighted in 1958 by ZIV Television Programs, Inc. produced under license from California National Productions, Inc.. Bat Masterson starred Gene Barry on the NBC television program.

Five colorful hand-screened Davy Crockett novelty sport shirts for boys.

Five hand painted Davy Crockett bow ties.

Novelty pajamas made of cotton flannel with Davy Crockett print. The label reads "Double Needle Creation by Nancy".

Three official Hopalong Cassidy knit pullover sweaters by Barclay. This particular boy's garment came packaged with the autographed picture of Hopalong Cassidy. The photo was copyrighted in 1949. The original price of the garment was $2.50.

Hopalong Cassidy novelty childrens' apparel fashionable in 1951.

Leather cowboy boots for boys popular in 1955.

Three pair of novelty western pajamas for the little buckaroo in green, yellow and blue cotton plisse. The label reads "Double-needle gowns, pajamas by Nancy".

Two-piece Matt Dillon Marshall Outfit with metal badge by Kaynee.

A wide assortment of novelty and western apparel for boys advertised as "...actually worn by Roy and his son Dusty on the Double R Bar Ranch", Sears, 1954.

Novelty western wear for boys was extremely fashionable in the 1950s, largely due to the popularity of the many TV westerns. Pictured here is a black cotton broadcloth shirt with official Hopalong Cassidy trademark on label and above pocket and Hopalong Cassidy buttons. The jersey gloves are marked Red Ryder and Rough Rider.

Hand-screened cotton tee-shirt featuring Roy Rogers and Trigger, label reads "Norwich". Also available in yellow.

Two cotton sweatshirts, fleece-lined, with hand-screened Howdy Doody design and original Bob Smith copyright. The label inside the garment reads "Norwich". The tag on the garment reads "It's Howdy Doody Time, It's Howdy Doody Time, Bob Smith and Howdy too, Say Howdy do to you." Copyright Bob Smith and Edward G. Kean, 1948.

Boy's western tee shirt featuring "The Lone Ranger and Silver" by Norwich.

Glossary

cetate - Synthetic fiber made of cellulose and acetic acid.

ngora - Silky yarn or cloth made from the hair of the Angora goat or Angora rabbit.

rgyle - Varicolored geometric patterns, especially diamond hapes, used in clothing, particularly knit socks and sweat-rs.

anlon - Tradename for the process that texturized yarn hich in turn, added stretch to certain synthetic fabrics.

atiste - A sheer fabric of plain weave, originally made of nen.

odice - Upper section of a woman's dress, more specifi-ally the portion between the shoulders and the waist.

oucle - A fabric that is either knitted or woven with a knot-ed or looped surface. Boucle is derived from the French ord Boucler, which means to curl or buckle.

roadcloth - A fabric of either mercerized cotton or spun ayon in which several warp yarns are woven together into fine crosswise rib.

rocade - Fabric used for clothing and/or decorating with aised or embossed floral or figural designs produced by weaving additional weft threads.

able knit - A decorative pattern used in knitted garments, specially sweaters, whereas the pattern resembles twisted ables.

apri pants - Italian-inspired pants for ladies with tapered egs, popular for summer wear.

ardigan - Long sleeve button-down sweater, either with -neck or rounded collar. In the 1950s, ladies' cardigan weaters were sometimes called Hollywood-style sweaters nd their counterparts for men were called coat sweaters.

ashmere - A fine, soft wool obtained from the undercoat f the Kashmir goat, found in the Himalayas. It was popu-arly used for sweaters, shawls, coats and suits.

hemise - A very simple loose-fitting garment, most com-nonly a dress, which hangs straight from the shoulders.

henille - A soft, furry or fuzzy fabric made of cotton, silk, vool or rayon yarn produced by weaving a cloth with warp nreads.

hiffon - A very lightweight, sheer fabric made of highly wisted single yarns of cotton, silk, wool, rayon or nylon,

very popular for evening wear.

Cotton - A popular fabric widely used in the manufacture of textiles made from the many yarns spun from the fibers of the cotton plant.

Crepe - A lightweight fabric of either cotton, rayon, silk, wool or synthetic, with a crinkled texture or surface.

Dacron - Tradename for a synthetic polyester fiber known for its great resilience and strength. In the 1950s, Dacron was known as a "Wonder Fiber" that was easily washable, quick drying and needed little or no ironing.

Damask - Similar to brocade cloth with woven designs but constructed thinner and finer and used for linens.

Embroidery - Decorative needlework on fabric, clothing or textiles done by hand or machine.

Faggoting - A type of embroidery in which threads are pulled and tied to form hourglass-shaped clusters or bundles.

Faille - A closely woven fabric made of rayon, cotton or silk with a semi-lustrous appearance, soft texture and a flat crosswise ribbed effect, similar to grosgrain.

Felt - An unwoven fabric made by a process of matting or interlocking fibers like wool, cotton, fur and rayon together using chemicals, heat, pressure or moisture forming a firm cloth. Felt was very popular used in millinery and for the wide circle skirts of the 1950s.

Flannel - Slightly napped, very soft fabric which is loosely woven used especially for sleepwear.

Foulard - Soft, lightweight, satiny fabric, usually silk or rayon, of twill or plain weave with printed designs. Primarily used for neckties, scarves and robes.

Frogging - A decorative fastening device made of braid which is commonly used on oriental-style garments.

Gabardine - A firm and durable rayon, cotton or wool fabric giving the appearance of diagonal ribs due to a tightly wo-ven twill weave. Gabardine was used extensively in the 1950s in the manufacture of suits for women and shirts for men.

Grosgrain - Silk or rayon fabric that is closely woven with crosswise or horizontal ribs.

Gusset - A piece of fabric, usually triangular or diamond-shaped, added to a garment usually in the underarm area, to increase strength and allow for movement.

Jacquard - A fabric woven on a jacquard loom, which weaves decorative patterns and intricate designs onto fab-ric being controlled by a punched paper strip. Popular ex-amples are brocades and damasks and seen in neckwear and lounging robes for men. It was named after the French inventor, Joseph M. Jacquard in 1834.

Jersey - A plain weft-knitted fabric of either cotton, rayon, silk, nylon, wool or synthetics, popular in the late 1950s.

Jodhpurs - Riding pants which are cut full around the hips and tight fitting from the knee down to the ankle.

Lamb's wool - Wool shorn from young sheep used for making sweaters.

Lamé - A brocade fabric in which gold and silver filling threads are woven to form a pattern or design used prima-rily for evening wear.

Linen - A strong, durable fabric made of flax fiber obtained from the flax plant, usually available in three weights.

Lycra - Synthetic fiber made by Du Pont in 1958.

Mandarin collar - Oriental-style stand-up collar used on dresses, jackets, coats and sometimes incorporating frog closures.

Mohair - A lustrous fabric in plain or twill weave made from the hair of the Angora goat.

Moiré - Fabric with a water-like or wave-like appearance usually made of silk or rayon, sometimes called watered silk.

Nylon - Tradename for a synthetic material made of polya-mides that are made from a dicarboxylic acid and a diamine, and characterized by its strength and elasticity. Nylon was the perfect choice for hoisery and also lingerie, summer dresses, blouses and shirts. Nylon was another "Wonder Fabric" of the 1950s since it is was quick drying, it hardly wrinkled, it was very durable and resisted moths and mil-

dew. Nylon was first introduced in 1938 by the DuPont Com-pany of Delaware and two years later nylon stockings were the height of fashion.

Organdy - A lightweight, transparent plain-woven muslin chemically treated for temporary or permanent stiffness.

Orlon - Tradename for a synthetic fiber woven from an acrylic resin. Orlon was a popular choice for cardigan sweat-ers for men, women and children in the 1950s. Orlon was also produced by DuPont.

Pedal-pushers - Loose-fitting slacks for women and girls, popular in the 1950s, that came just below the knees, some-times made with cuffs.

Peplum - A ruffle, flounce or short over-skirt attached at the waist or bodice of a dress, jacket or blouse.

Plisse - A fabric, usually of cotton, that is given a perma-nent puckered or crinkled appearance by treating it with a caustic soda solution. It is most often used for sleepwear made in colorful and whimsical prints.

Polished cotton - Plain-weave cotton with a glazed or shiny finish.

Puckered nylon - Lightweight fabric, sometimes transpar-ent, made by weaving pre-shrunk and non-shrunk nylon yarns together.

Rayon - The first synthetic fiber chemically made from cel-lulose. Rayon is a shiny fabric that closely resembles silk.

Satin - A thick-textured glossy fabric made of silk, cotton, rayon or acetate, used primarily for evening wear and lin-ings.

Shantung - Silk or blended fabric in plain weave having a slightly irregular surface due to uneven filling yarns of wild silk.

Sharkskin - Smooth fabric of wool, silk, rayon or synthetic with a shiny surface and textured weave.

Shirring - Two or more rows of gathers on a garment used for decorative purposes.

Silk - Natural fiber produced from silkworms.

Smocking - Gathering and stitching of fabric for decorative purposes, commonly applied to little girls' dresses.

Spandex - Synthetic fiber introduced by Du Pont in 1958 characterized by its strength and elasticity. It was a good choice for swimwear and foundation garments.

Stiletto - Italian high-heeled shoes popular in the 1950s.

Stirrup pants - Close-fitting pants with a strap that fits un-der the foot. They were extremely fashionable in the 1950s and again in the 1980s.

Taffeta - A silk, linen, rayon or synthetic fabric made with a plain weave and a fine cross rib. Taffeta has a shiny, lus-trous and smooth appearance.

Trapeze Line - A clothing style popular in 1958 credited to Yves St. Laurent.

Tricot - Plain weave fabric made of silk, rayon, wool or cot-ton being made either sheer or opaque and popularly used for sleepwear or undergarments.

Tulle - Named after the city in France where it was origi-nally made, tulle is a stiff net made with a hexagonal mesh construction, usually of rayon, silk, or nylon. It was primarily used for ballet costumes, veils, prom and evening gowns.

Velvet - A silk, cotton, nylon, wool or rayon fabric with a short weave forming a smooth, soft fabric.

Velveteen - Fabric that resembles velvet, made of cotton, in plain or twill weaves.

Voile - A lightweight, sheer, plain weave fabric similar to organdy with good draping qualities and popular for sum-mer dresses.

Waffle cloth - A textured cotton with a honeycomb weave, woven on a dobby loom.

Warp - The lengthwise threads of a woven fabric.

Weft - Thread that crosses the warp and extends from sal-vage to salvage.

Yoke - Top section of a garment, the portion that runs across the bust and around the back.

Bibliography

BOOKS

Dorner, Jane. *Fashion In The Forties and Fifties.* New Rochelle, New York: Arlington House Publishers, 1975.

Dyer, Rod and Ron Spark. *Fit To Be Tied, Vintage Ties of the Forties & Early Fifties.* New York: Abbeville Press Publishers, 1987.

Kennett, Frances. *The Collectors Book of Fashion.* New York: Crown Publishers, Inc., 1983.

O'Hara, Georgina. *The Encyclopedia of Fashion.* New York: Harry N. Abrams, Inc. Publishers, 1986.

CATALOGS

Aldens, Chicago, Illinois, Spring and Summer, 1959.

Montgomery Ward, Chicago, Illinois, Spring and Summer 1953, Spring and Summer 1955, Spring and Summer 1957.

National Bellas Hess, Spring and Summer 1955.

Sears, Roebuck & Company, Philadelphia and Chicago, Spring and Summer 1951, Fall and Winter 1953, Christmas 1954, Spring and Summer 1955, Fall and Winter 1958.

Spiegel, Chicago, Illinois, Spring and Summer 1948, Spring and Summer 1951.

MAGAZINES

Family Circle (September 1956, October 1958, November 1958).

Glamour (August 1954).

Harper's Bazaar (August 1957).

Seventeen (November 1958).

Vogue (October 1955).

Woman's Day (September 1958).

Woman's Home Companion (March 1953 and March 1956).

Price Guide

(Original advertisements are not priced).

CHAPTER 1
FASHIONS FOR WOMEN

DRESSES

COTTON HOUSE DRESSES

Basic prints	20-35
Novelty prints	40-65
Sundresses	25-35
w/bolero jackets	35-50
Wraparound dresses	25-35

RAYON DRESSES

Printed rayon	50-90
w/beadwork	75-125
Linen-like rayon	30-50
w/decoration	45-65
Gabardine Dresses	40-60
w/decoration	65-95
Silk Dresses	75-100
w/beadwork	150-200
Nylon Dresses	40-60
Chiffon Dresses	50-75
w/beadwork	75-125
Taffeta Dresses	65-85
w/decoration	100-200
Satin Dresses	75-100
w/jackets	100-150
w/beadwork	150-200
Velvet Dresses	75-100
w/beadwork or rhinestones	125-175

SUITS

Gabardine suits	75-150
Rayon suits	75-125
Cotton suits	60-85
Lilli Ann suit (p38)	150-200
Sweater suits	40-60
w/beadwork	75-100

SKIRTS

Felt circle skirts	45-65
w/decorations	60-90
Cotton circle skirts	
Basic prints	20-35
Novelty prints	40-65
Straight skirts	25-45
Pleated skirts	25-45

BLOUSES

Cotton blouses	
Sleeveless	10-20
w/decorations	20-30
Short sleeve	15-25
w/decorations	25-35
Nylon blouses	20-30
w/decorations	25-35
Rayon blouses	25-35
w/decorations	35-45
Lace blouses	30-40
w/decorations	35-45
Silk blouses	35-50
w/beadwork	50-100

CARDIGAN SWEATERS

Orlon	15-25
w/decorations	35-50
Wool	40-60
w/fur trim	65-95
w/beadwork	75-100
Cashmere	50-90
w/beadwork	75-100
Sweater Shrugs	20-30
w/beadwork	35-45

PULLOVERS

Orlon	15-25
w/beadwork	25-35
Rayon boucle	30-40

ROBES

Crinkle cotton	30-50
Quilted cotton	35-60
Quilted acetate	40-65
Chenille	75-100
Silk	75-125

NIGHT GOWNS

Cotton Plisse	18-25
Rayon	25-40

PAJAMAS

Rayon	25-45
Satin	45-65
Cotton	20-30

CHAPTER 2
FASHIONS FOR YOUNG WOMEN AND GIRLS

COTTON DRESSES

Basic prints	15-20
Novelty prints	25-35
Nylon	20-30
w/decorations	25-35

SWEATERS

Cardigans	8-12
w/decorations	12-20
Shrugs	8-10
w/decorations	10-15
Coat & Bonnet sets	50-75
Pedal pusher sets	15-20
Short sets	10-15

Denim jeans	35-45

ROBES

Quilted cotton	25-35
Chenille	30-40

PAJAMAS

Cotton plisse	
Basic prints	10-15
Novelty prints	15-25
Flannel	
Basic prints	12-18
Novelty prints	18-25

CHAPTER 3
FASHIONS FOR MEN

RAYON SHIRTS

Hawaiian	45-75
Casual shirts	30-40
Dress shirts	40-65

COTTON SHIRTS

Casual shirts	25-40
Dress shirts	35-50

GABARDINE SHIRTS

Casual shirts	35-50
Dress shirts	45-65

NYLON SHIRTS 20-30

PULLOVERS

Cable Knit	35-50
Rayon & Acetate	25-40
Combed cotton	20-30
Denim jeans	75-150

ROBES

Short	50-75
Long	75-125
Neckties	20-50
Socks	3-5
Leather Belts	10-20
Boxer shorts	
Basic prints	3-5
Novelty prints	5-10

CHAPTER 3
FASHIONS FOR YOUNG MEN AND BOYS

Sport Denim sets	50-75

ırdigan sweaters	25-50
IIRTS	
ɪtton	
:asual shirts	10-15
ɪress shirts	15-25
ıyon	
:asual shirts	15-20
ɪress shirts	20-30
ınnel	
ɪasic prints	15-20
ovelty prints	20-35
·nim jeans	50-75
ILLOVERS	
ombed cotton	15-20
able knit	20-30
ɪtriped polo	6-10
'LON SHIRTS	
ɪuckered	12-18
ɪrinted	18-25
IESS SHIRTS	
/cuff links	20-25
/cuff links &	
ɔw ties	25-35
ort sets	25-35
.bardine jackets	30-40
ow suits	50-75
ɪstern outfit	
ɪodhpurs	75-100
sure suits	50-75
acon Robes	50-75
JAMAS	
ɪrinkle cotton	12-18
annel	18-25
ɪckties	10-25
ɪw ties	8-15
ɔks	1-3
ɪer shorts	2-5

ɪSTERN CLOTHING

ɪTTON SHIRTS	
ɔ-toned	
/decorations	40-65
ɪnd-screened	40-60
.nnel	35-55
ɔby Benson	60-85

BAT MASTERSON OUTFITS	100-150
MATT DILLON OUTFITS	100-150
DAVY CROCKETT	
Shirts	50-75
Bow ties	15-20
Pajamas	30-40
HOPALONG CASSIDY	
Sweaters w/ pictures	225-300
Broadcloth shirt	125-200
Red Rider gloves	25-35
Rough Rider gloves	15-25
Roy Rogers shirt	30-40
Lone Ranger shirt	35-45
Howdy Doody sweatshirts	40-65

Index

Back Cover Photo, BR: The Etting family Terry, Roseann, Clint, Ambe and Alexandra dressed in fifties' fash ions. *Photo by Roger Schoch*